dance the line
paintings by
karl benjamin

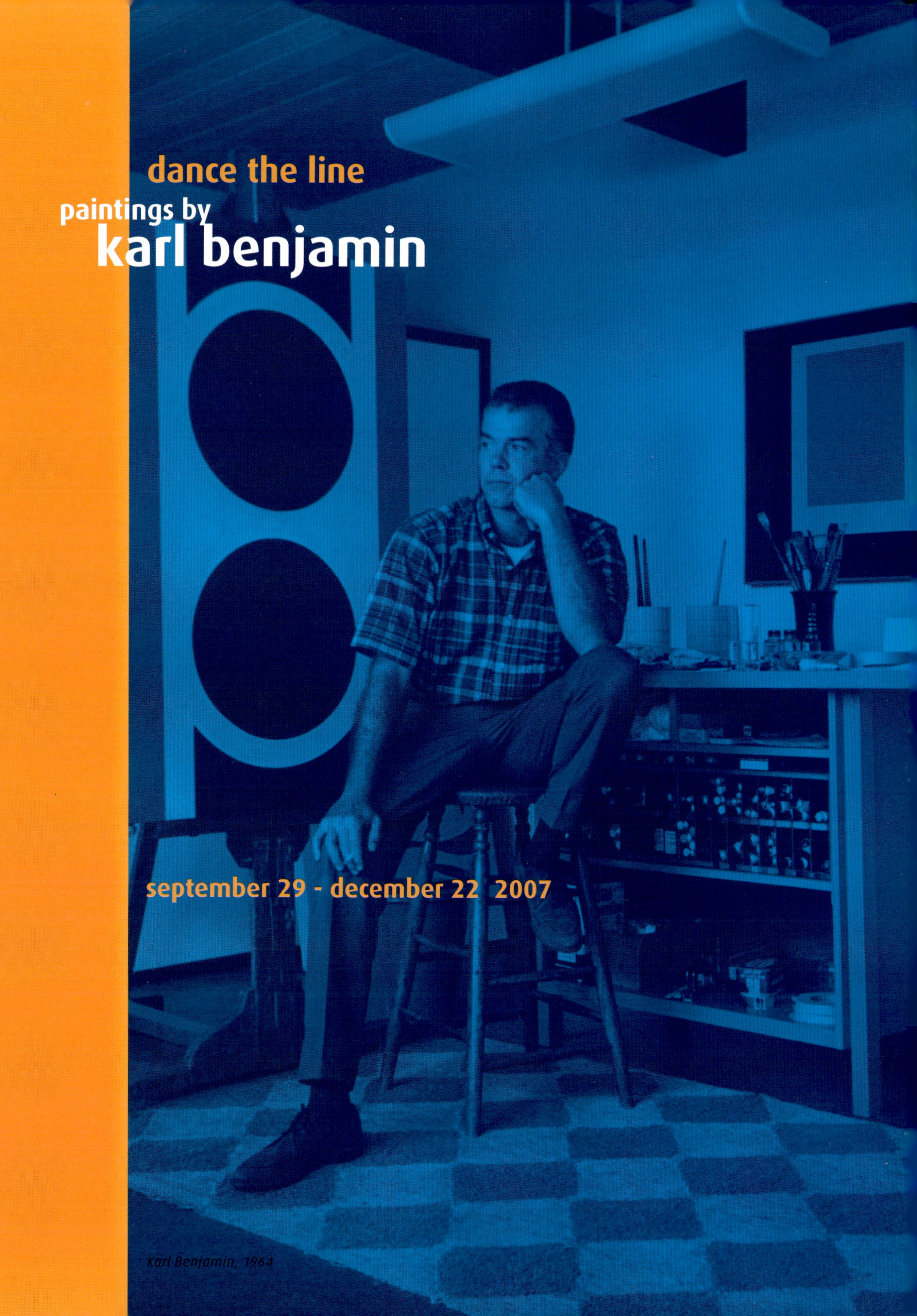

dance the line
paintings by
karl benjamin
september 29 - december 22 2007
Karl Benjamin, 1964

contents

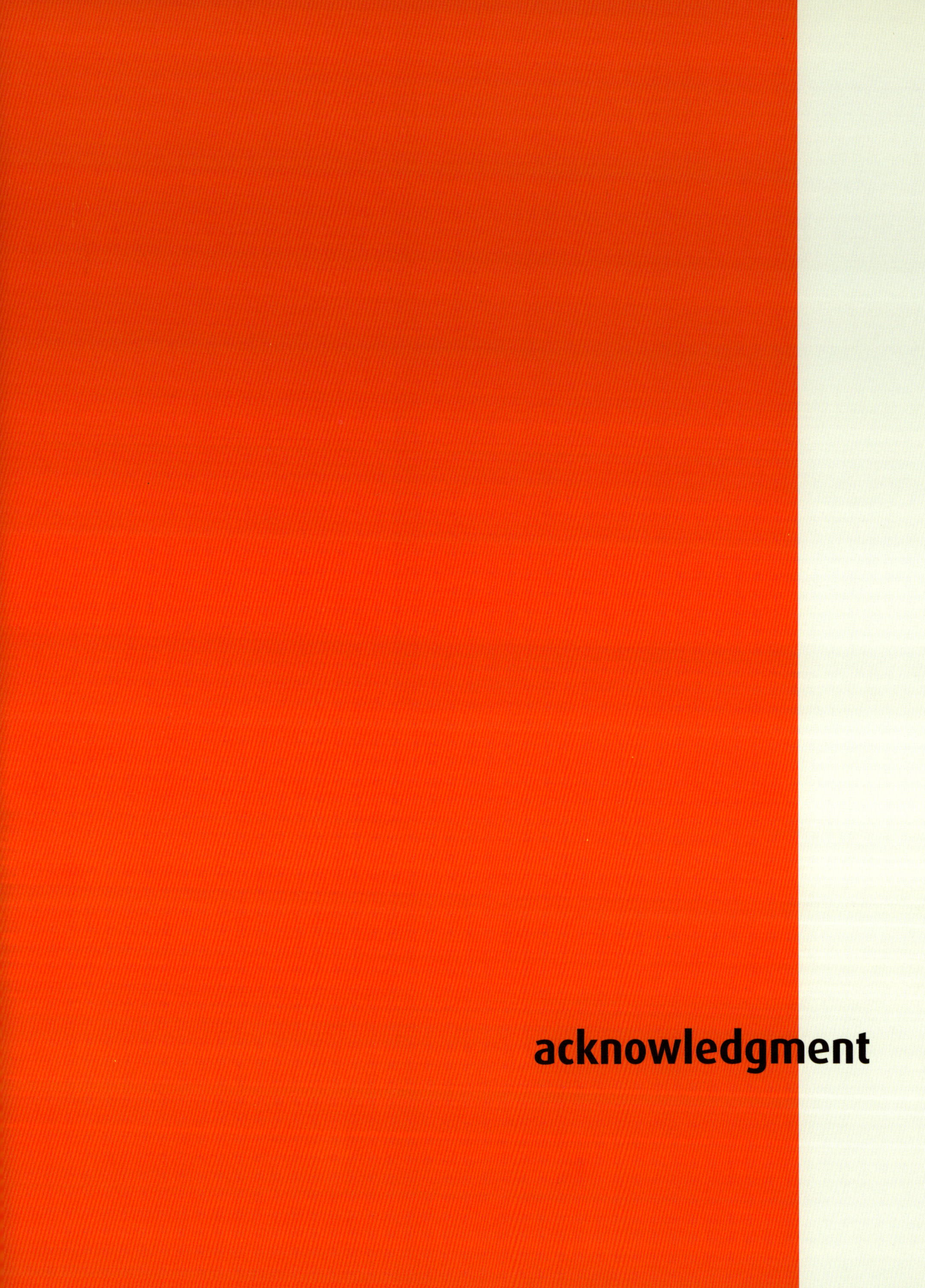

acknowledgment

Good things come to those who wait, or so the saying goes. I believe that the wait is over for Karl Benjamin and "good things" are finally truly here.

This catalogue, spanning Benjamin's almost fifty year career, celebrates the scope, power and sheer beauty of his œuvre. It seems remarkable that given his art-making discipline, he should only just now be getting his due. Karl's work has long been beloved by those of us who were aware of the past half-century's groundbreaking Southern California art scene.

Karl's rise to his current level of national and international prominence is one of the most truly earned trajectories on record. Helping to create this scenario has been one of the single greatest pleasures of my long career in the art business. I am honored to be involved in the creation of this exhibition and production of this catalogue as well as the re-examination and renaissance of Southern California's Geometric Abstraction better known as Hard Edge painting.

First and foremost I want to thank Karl for creating this extraordinary body of work. I also want to acknowledge his continued support and enthusiasm for the gallery's endeavors on his behalf. Karl's energy and insights have inspired us all. It is a privilege to know him and a pleasure to represent him.

I would also like to offer a special word of thanks to Bob Jones, Karl's son-in-law. His patience, good humor and willingness to serve as our hands and eyes in Karl's "atelier" have been invaluable.

Steve Comba, Assistant Director/Registrar of the Pomona College Museum of Art and Curator of Karl's recent retrospective at the new Claremont Museum of Art, has been of tremendous help.

I want to express my thanks again to Barry Berkus, who had the foresight to introduce me to Karl's work.

It is always a profound delight to read anything written by Dave Hickey. He has long been a champion of this work and I am honored to have him on our team and our pages.

This acknowledgment would not be complete without a grateful nod to Karl's better half, Beverly. She has simply been the best.

Finally, I would like to thank my staff, Jenise Ramos and Michelle Bahk, for their yeoman efforts in preparing this publication and my gallery director, Marie Chambers, for orchestrating it all.

Louis Stern

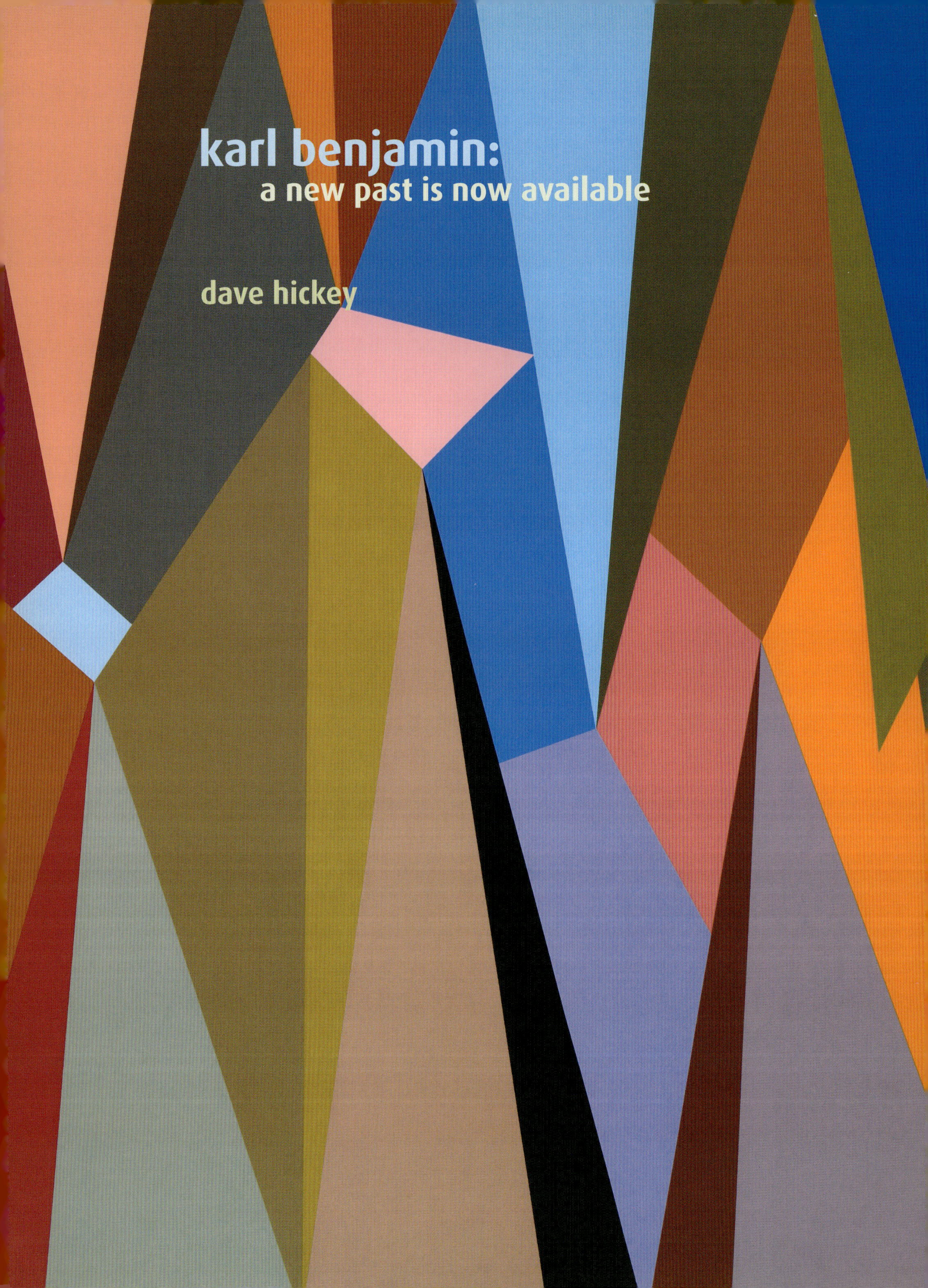
karl benjamin:
a new past is now available
dave hickey

When I was a kid, we lived in Pacific Palisades in a house that hung off the cliff overlooking the Pacific. Eventually, years later, that house would slide down onto the PCH, but we were long gone by then. During those years, I wanted to surf, that was it. I wanted to haul my clunky board up and down the concrete steps leading to the beach, sometimes, out of sheer exhaustion, sliding my board on the stair-rails. My Dad wanted me to listen to jazz or, more precisely, he didn't want me to bother him while he listened 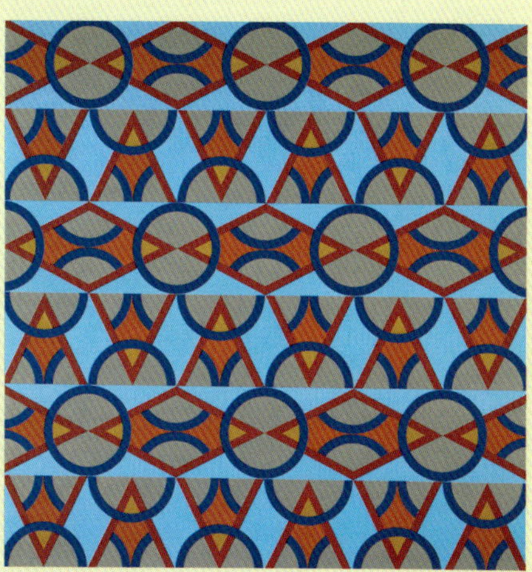 to jazz. I didn't mind this. I would even ride with him down to Hermosa Beach to the Lighthouse where one could listen to jazz in one's wet bathing trunks. My Mom wanted me to ride all over Los Angeles with her looking for art, up to Hollywood, out to Pasadena, to San Marino, and over to Claremont. When we found some art (usually hanging on white pegboard wall with an adjacent rubber plant), we would look at it. I resisted these trips mightily but, as it turned out, I was never more than a B- surfer and at best a B+ musician. I was, however, an A+ looker at art.

So, even then, as unwilling as I was to traipse around, I still had my favorites. I liked the hardedge stuff by Fred Hammersley, Karl Benjamin, and John McLaughlin. It reminded me, somehow, in its apparent effortlessness, of the claritas of surfing where one must never be seen to be trying very hard. My Mom, who had a darker vision of the world, liked Rico LeBrun and other artists whose work looked like it hurt to make. She said I would learn when I grew up but I never did. Even so, I have to thank her here for the privilege I have today, of writing in my maturity, about the first art I liked as a feckless youth, especially for the pleasure of visiting a career that has paralleled my own at one remove. Not many of one's youthful enthusiasm survive with us into adulthood, of course, so I am embarrassed to this day about Colin Wilson, Herman Hesse and George Battaile. *On the Road*, however, is still a great book and Karl Benjamin is still a great painter, not just a neglected local, not just a victim of fashion's whim, but a genuine world class practitioner who has, as they say in Georgia, hoed his own row.

Having grown up in an art world replete with stunted careers, bitterly disappointed halfwits and professores who have abandoned all hope, this is a glorious occasion for me. It's also comforting to realize that Benjamin, Hammersley and McLaughlin, after their fifteen minutes of international fame as "Abstract Classicists," in Los Angeles, San Francisco, New York and London, continued to flourish in the sunshine of absolute neglect, produced steadily, and created substantial bodies of work that we embrace now with amazement and a little twinge of shame for not having noticed. The volume and variety of this work, today, is a little overwhelming. Reviewing Benjamin's half-century of work for the first time is like stepping into Ali Baba's cave or King Tut's tomb. You want more time, and wish you had had more occasions over the years since the vast array speaks to us, in its refinement and complexity, of older, more rigorous, habits of production. It embodies a very different conception of the artist's vocation, which, unfortunately, for pigeonhole-art-historians, has nothing to do with Abstract Classicism---the term with which curator Jules Langsner saddled Karl Benjamin, John McLaughlin, Frederick Hammersley and Lorser Feitelson and to which they all objected---although not so strenuously as to undermine the exhibition that made their reputations.

Far from being Classicists, my favorites were all odd ducks and elegant urban gentleman. John McLaughlin was always the cagy, elliptical Zen master, Hammersley, the subtle, genteel, and muscular wit, and Benjamin, always, the sybaritic Hellenist, aghast at the infinity of options that his brand of oil painting promised. Lorser Feitelson, the fourth Abstract Classicist, was a wonderful painter, but never so cool and American as the other three, nor ever as joyful. Even today, I can think of no other artist whose paintings exude the joy and pleasure of being an artist with more intensity than Karl Benjamin's nor any other artist whose long teaching career has left no blemish of cynicism on his practice. He is always the kid in the candy store, the kid with the rock in his pocket drawing it out, showing it to you and exclaiming "Wow! Look at this." As a consequence, the shape of Benjamin's practice, driven by rigorous hedonistic curiosity, more closely resembles that of a younger generation of California artists than that of his peers. Like Edward Ruscha, Billy Al Bergsten and Peter Alexander, Benjamin doesn't follow a path, deal with issues or aspire to a "look." The narrative of Benjamin's work spreads like a delta.

A variegated bouquet of visual opportunities are addressed, explored, set aside, and returned to when they interest him again. There are multiple situations to which he returns and departs at will. Some of Benjamin's paintings speak to the moment of their creation. (There are wonderful 50's paintings that evoke the populuxe curves and iconic

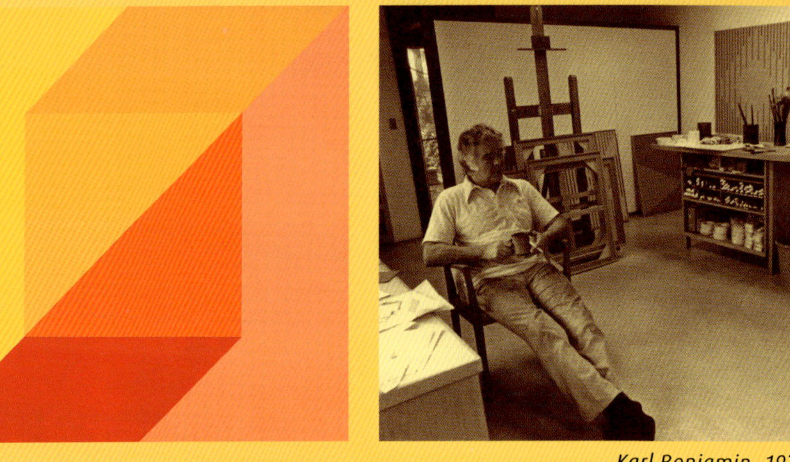

Karl Benjamin, 1978

modernity of that era.) There are other paintings that seem grounded in memory, in a recollection of missed exits or roads not taken. Some seem intended to respond to the challenge of other artist's work. There are large grids and the small grids, wallpaper patterns and fields of irregularly conjoined triangles; there are stripes, horizontal and vertical, unfurling sequences of angled panels, and a whole array of signature elements that allude to designed objects, maps and stylized landscapes. Amidst this community of preferred formats there are singular objects, as well, that relate to nothing else. Throughout his career Benjamin has moved from one of these ongoing projects to the next as the mood strikes him with incidental one-of-a-kind inventions inserted for punctuation (this being the privilege of not having a dealer whispering in your ear).

All of Benjamin's linear arrays become settings for chromatic invention. The array of lines in the rectangle comes first, and provides the occasion for color solutions, but, even so, chicken-egg arguments about the relative precedence of color and line, figure and ground dissolve into pleasurable confusion. If there is a rule at work in these paintings it is, as Benjamin has remarked, to shun no color, and, as a result, there is no other painter with whom I am familiar, who can deploy and totally de-naturalize the browns, greens, grays and burgundies of the natural world with more acuity, usually by juxtaposing them with zinging violets and burning yellow-reds.

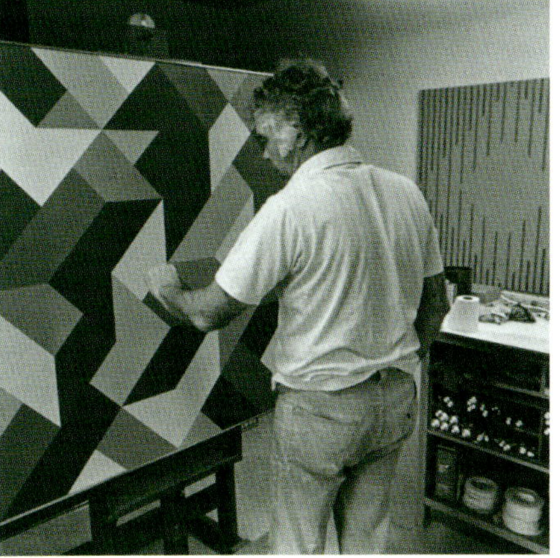

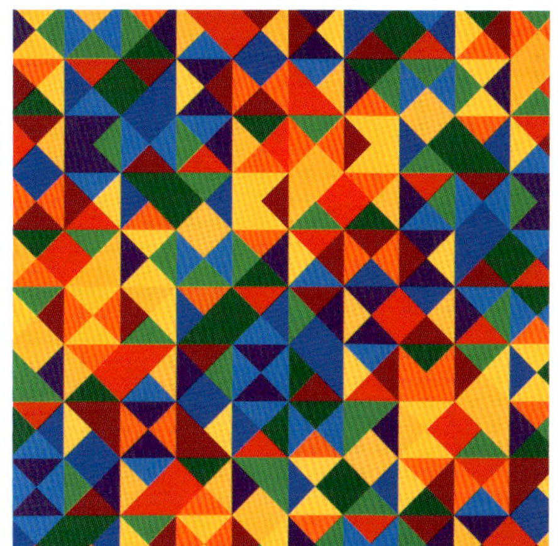

As a result, no green in Benjamin alludes to foliage; no brown alludes to the dirt in which the foliage grows. Benjamin takes these hues, burdened as they are with primal references, and makes them back into free colors, live presences. This is no small achievement and the physical consequences of his axiom to shun no color, speak directly to Gerhard Richter's proposition that "all abstract painting is an allegory of social relations." For Benjamin, the fact that no color is excluded and all colors are highly individualized, graded and nuanced by context is, in itself, a vision of the world and of society in its specificity---expressed in a world of color so specified that I actually made a short tour through Benjamin's oeuvre looking for standard stuff---for "paint-card" colors and "color wheel" hues. I found one orange triangle that looked pretty standard. That was it.

My point here is that, since the quality and quantity of Benjamin's oeuvre has never been at issue, we must look elsewhere for explanations of his burgeoning vogue. The primary reason, I think, for the reconsideration of Benjamin and all of his brothers-in-arms has to be the rising tide of globalism and the gradual recession of New York City as a center of influence. The first consequence of this recession has been to remove New York School painting from the vortex, from its hegemonic position as the supreme pivot in the history of twentieth century art. One need only consider Abstract Expressionism, for just a moment, as just another style to see with a great deal of clarity that, in the Post World War II period, Geometric Abstraction, or Op Art, or Hard Edge painting, or whatever you want to call it was, in fact, the dominant global idiom of that era, the true cosmopolitan language of post war art. During this era,

Helio Oittica in Brazil, Raphael Soto in Venezuela, Max Bill in Germany, Jo Baer in New York, Bridget Riley in Britain, Victor Vasarely in Paris, Benjamin, McLaughlin and Hammersley in Los Angeles and hundreds of other artists created a massive body of work, which, if considered collectively, provides a much more rational precedent for the Puritanical Minimalism that followed in New York and the Hedonistic Minimalism that followed in Los Angeles.

As a consequence of this revised perspective, there have been literally hundreds of exhibitions in the last five years that address the new landscape that has revealed itself with the demotion of Abstract Expressionism. Geometric shows, Minimalist shows, Op shows, Hard Edge shows have been mounted all over the world. This is historicizing work that does what public museums should do. It reconsiders work that has fallen from fashion but not from intellectual esteem. The revival, of course, has also been driven by the sheer force of attrition occasioned by a booming art market. Most prominently, however, I would suggest, the revival of interest in geometric abstraction from the past has been driven by a flourishing practice of geometric abstraction in the present by young artists who have fallen back upon this work as a source of inspiration---as a starting point outside the hegemony of fashion. Citing my own experience I can attest to the fact that, in the mid nineteen nineties, I suddenly had students who kept scrapbooks of Polaroids of this work, who called collectors to visit works that were unavailable in public museums. Suddenly, artists in their seventies were receiving studio visits from artists in their twenties.

I must note here that, in my perception, this vogue among young artists was less a paradigm shift than a reconsideration of just exactly how an artist should live. The possibility of stepping outside academia and the realm of public patronage, of spending one's time working in a studio became attractive again. As a consequence, something very special happened that is relatively unprecedented in the history of American art. Young artists began seeking not just mentors in the past, but colleagues. They perceived in the practice of geometric abstraction an incomplete project. So they wanted to see shows organized around the flourishing of geometric abstraction as an international language, but most of all, they wanted to show with these older artists. They wanted to hang their works in the same room with Benjamin, Hammersley, Riley, and Soto and test their chops. The result has been what I call "grandparental" exhibitions in which young and old artists with formal affinities exhibit together. I mounted a show of this sort myself, called Beau Monde, in Santa Fe, the critic David Pagel and painter Jim Hayward have also mounted a-historical shows of this sort in Claremont and Los Angeles. Others are springing up all over the world, in Buffalo, Cologne, Brussels, etc. Galleries now sport stables that include artists regardless of generation who share

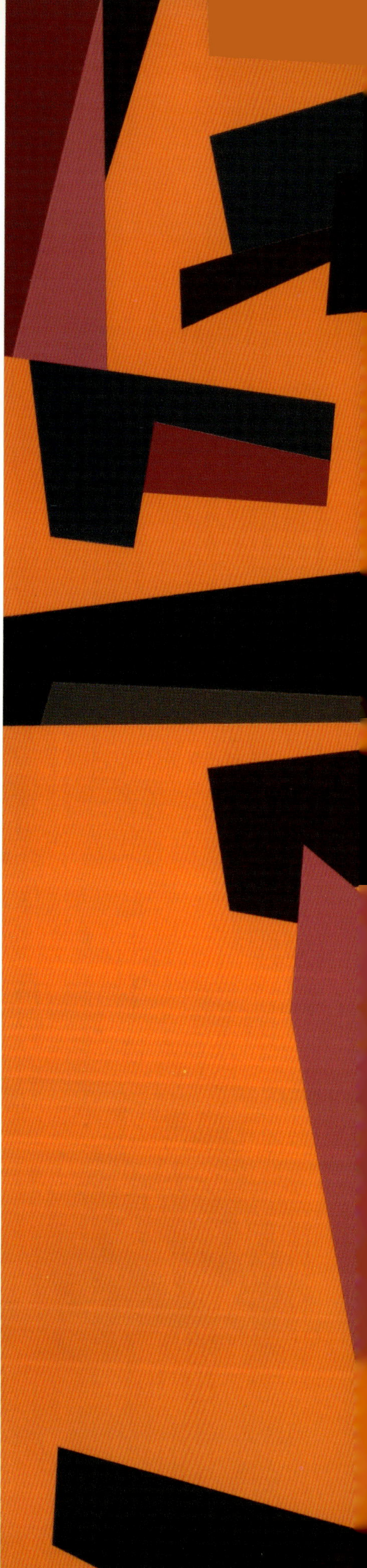

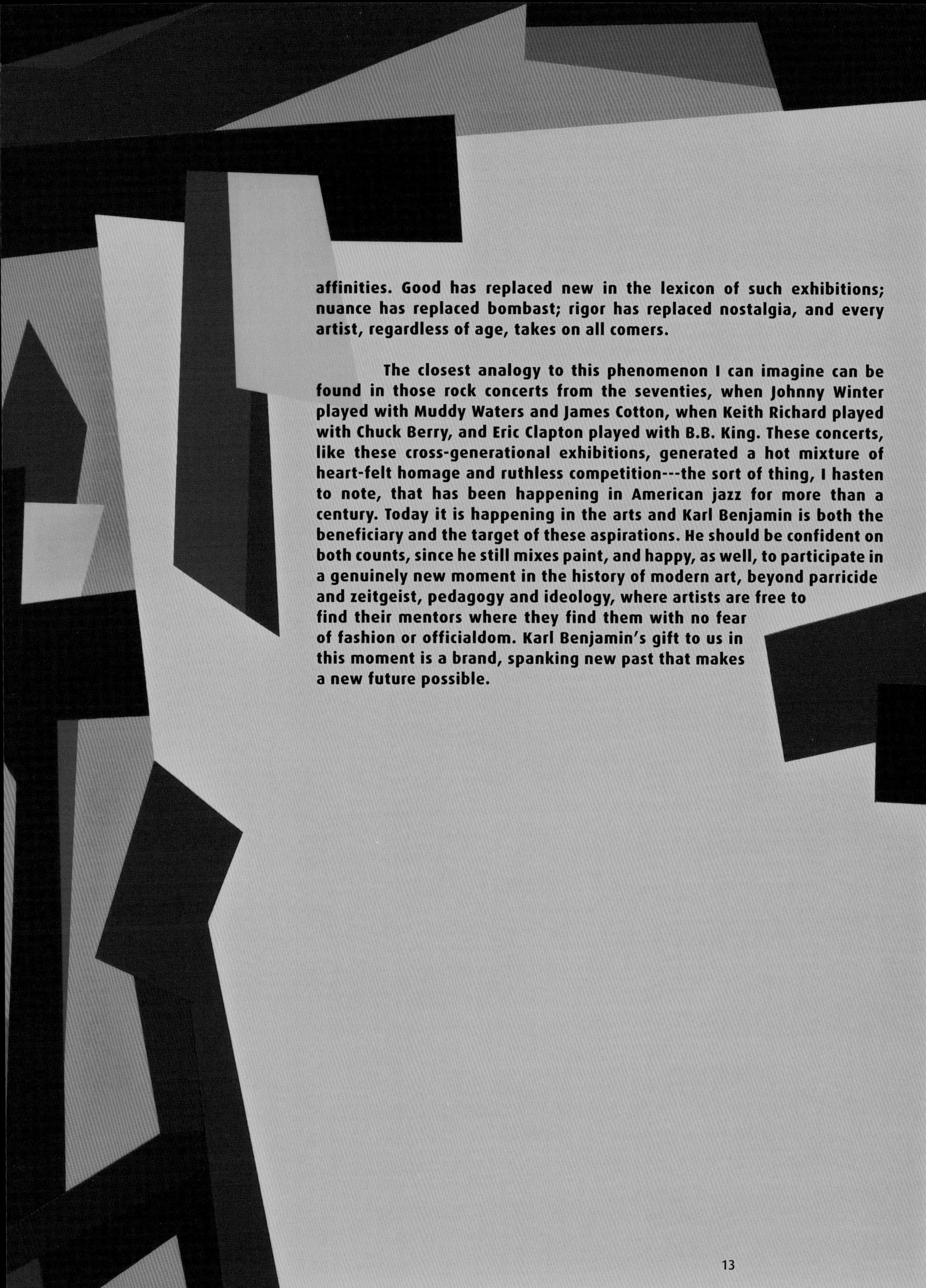

affinities. Good has replaced new in the lexicon of such exhibitions; nuance has replaced bombast; rigor has replaced nostalgia, and every artist, regardless of age, takes on all comers.

The closest analogy to this phenomenon I can imagine can be found in those rock concerts from the seventies, when Johnny Winter played with Muddy Waters and James Cotton, when Keith Richard played with Chuck Berry, and Eric Clapton played with B.B. King. These concerts, like these cross-generational exhibitions, generated a hot mixture of heart-felt homage and ruthless competition---the sort of thing, I hasten to note, that has been happening in American jazz for more than a century. Today it is happening in the arts and Karl Benjamin is both the beneficiary and the target of these aspirations. He should be confident on both counts, since he still mixes paint, and happy, as well, to participate in a genuinely new moment in the history of modern art, beyond parricide and zeitgeist, pedagogy and ideology, where artists are free to find their mentors where they find them with no fear of fashion or officialdom. Karl Benjamin's gift to us in this moment is a brand, spanking new past that makes a new future possible.

plates

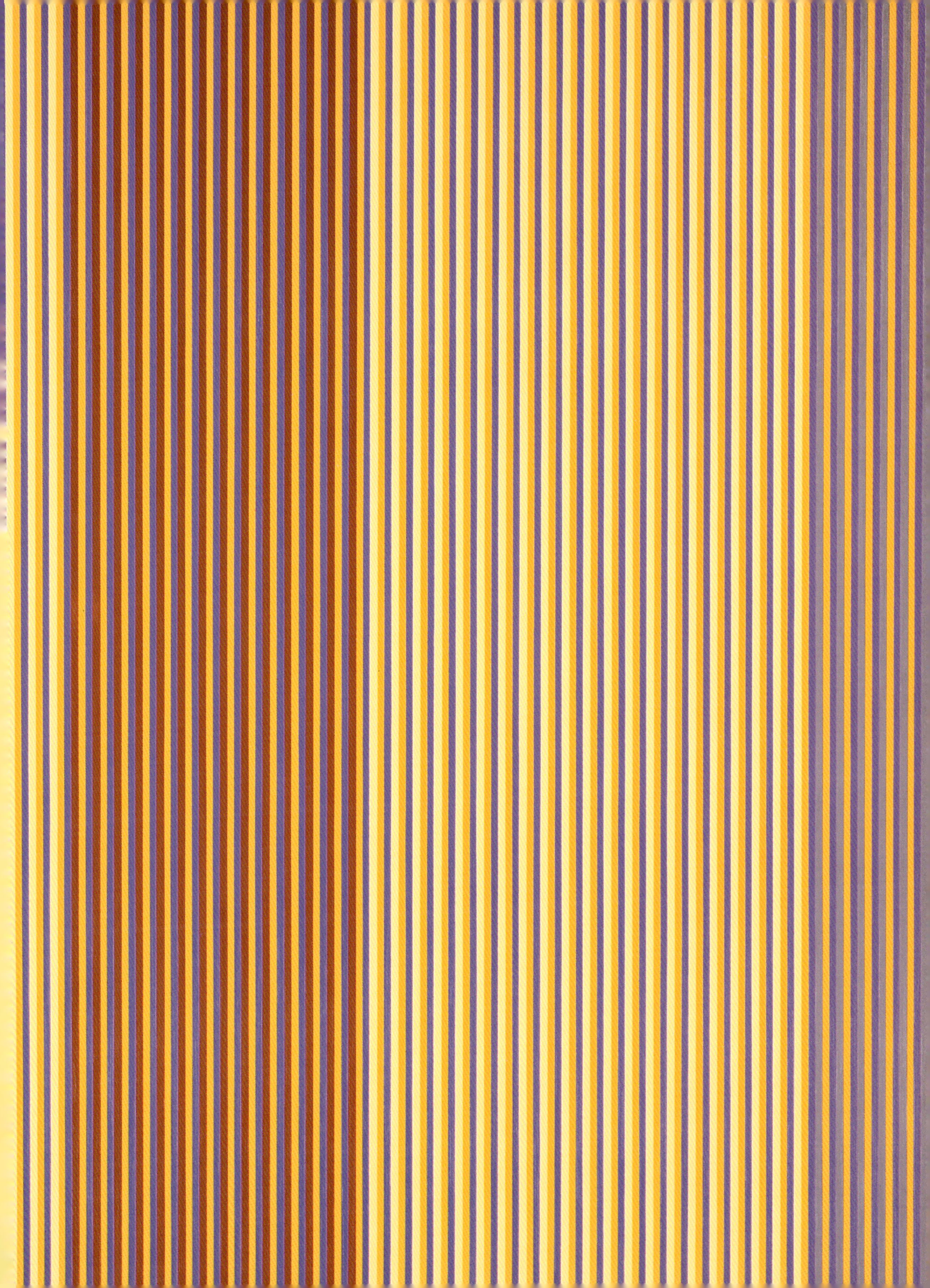

1 **jagged landscape with sun**

1954
oil on canvas
24 x 40 inches
61 x 101.6 centimeters

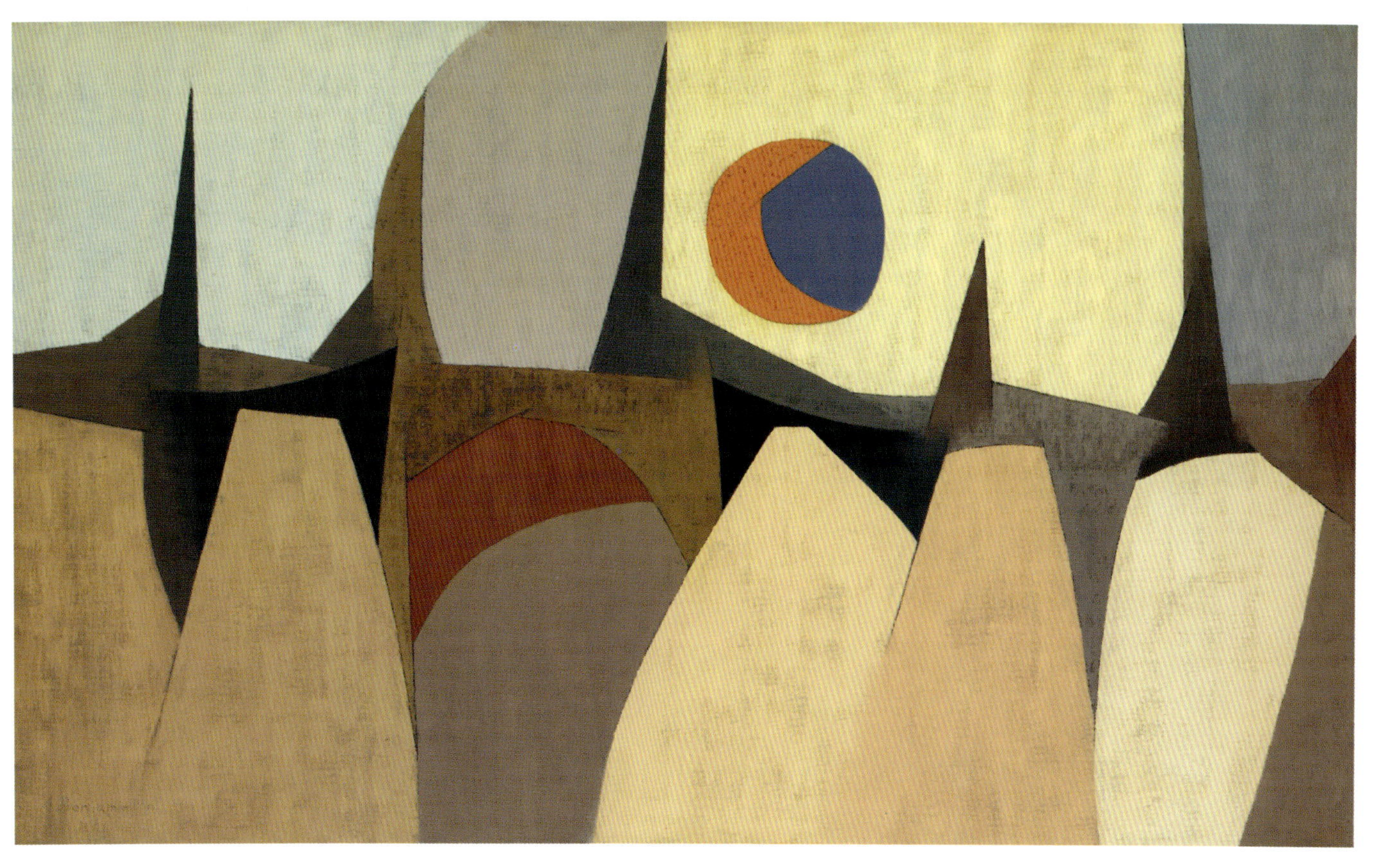

2 **stage II**

1958
oil on canvas
50 x 70 inches
127 x 177.8 centimeters

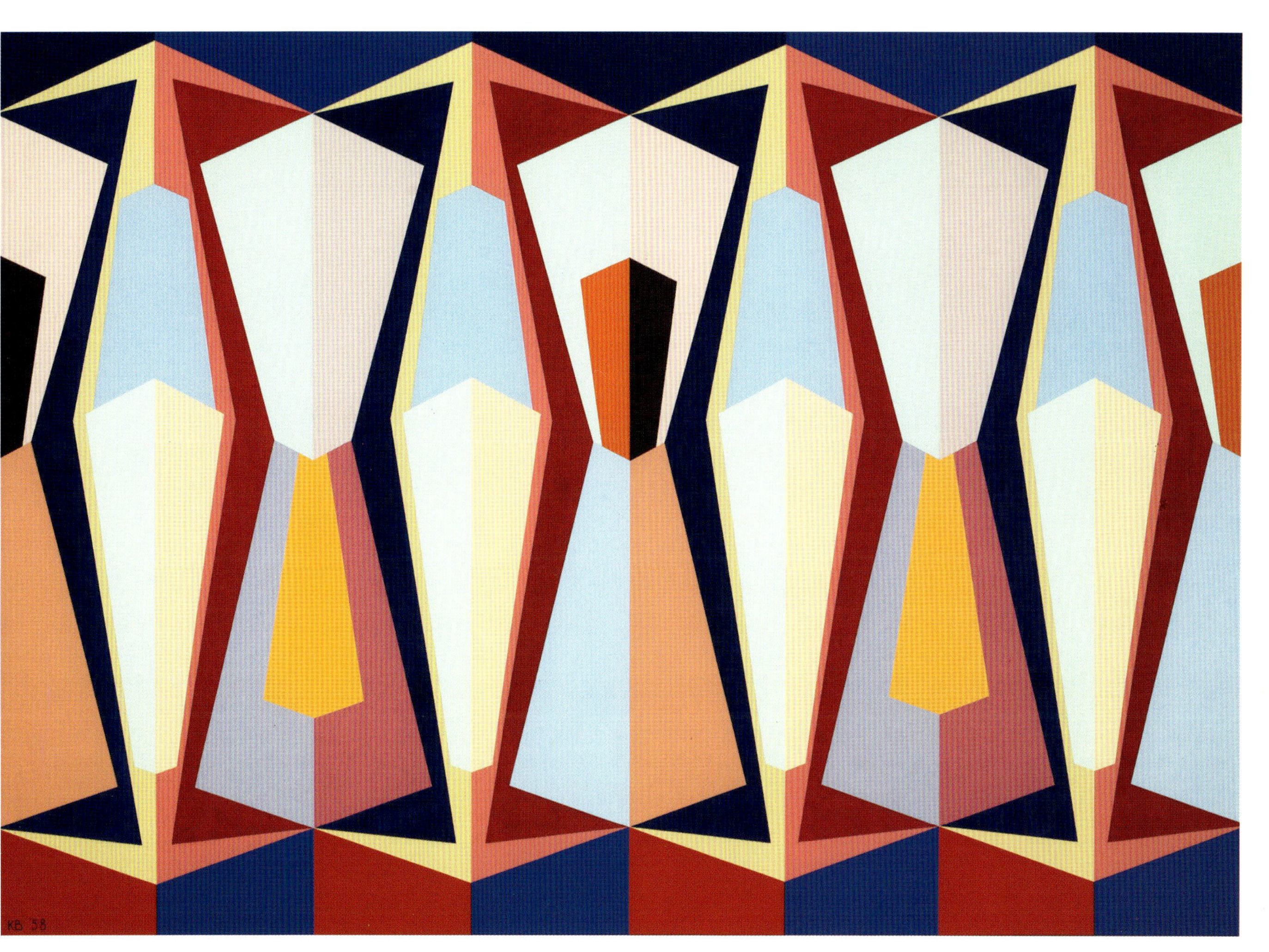

**interlocking forms
(thalo green, raw umber, mars yellow)**

1958
oil on canvas
40 x 30 inches
101.6 x 76.2 centimeters

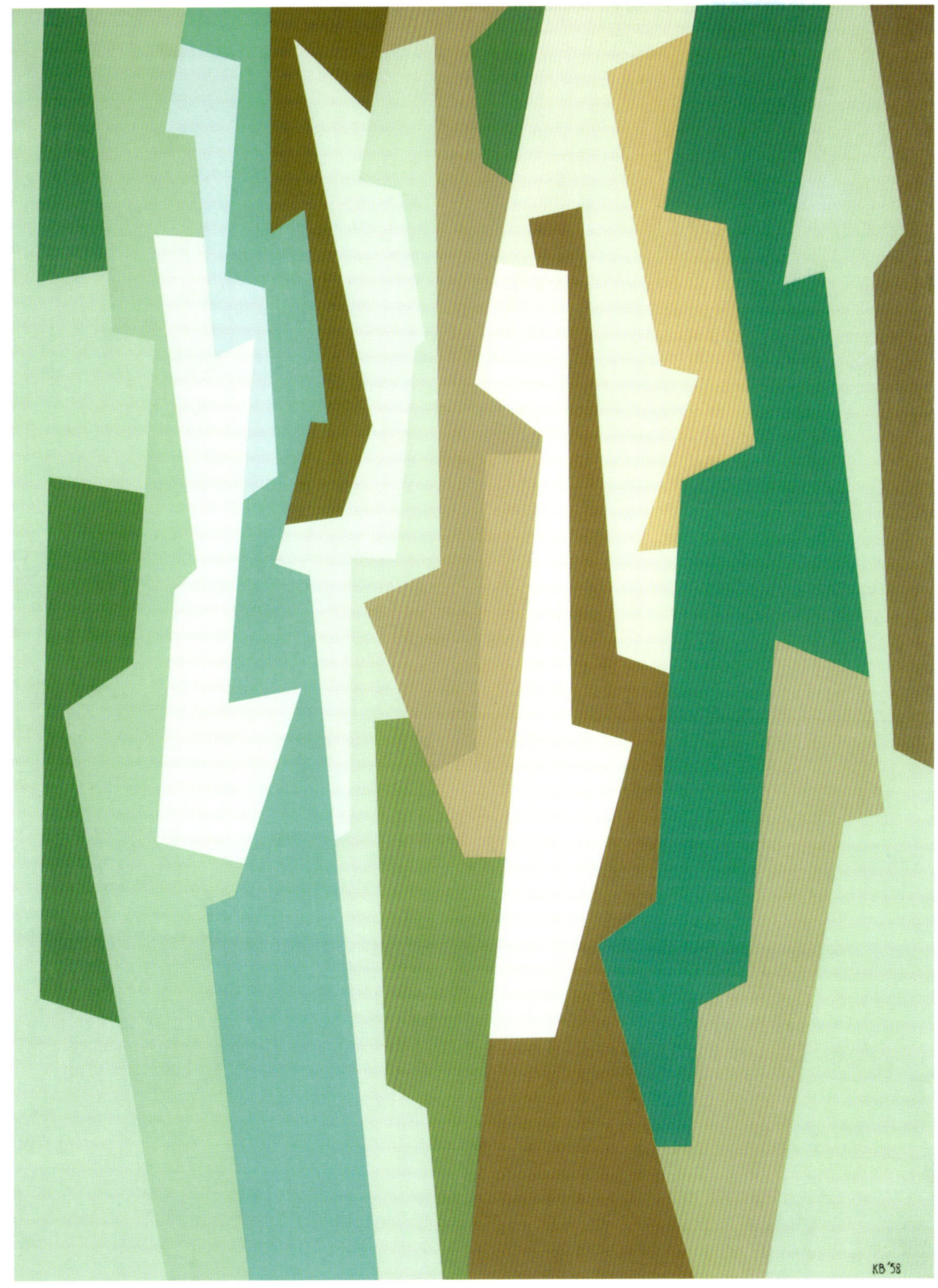

KB '58

4 interlocking forms
(amber, umber, yellow, crimson)

1959
oil on canvas
40 x 50 inches
101.6 x 127 centimeters

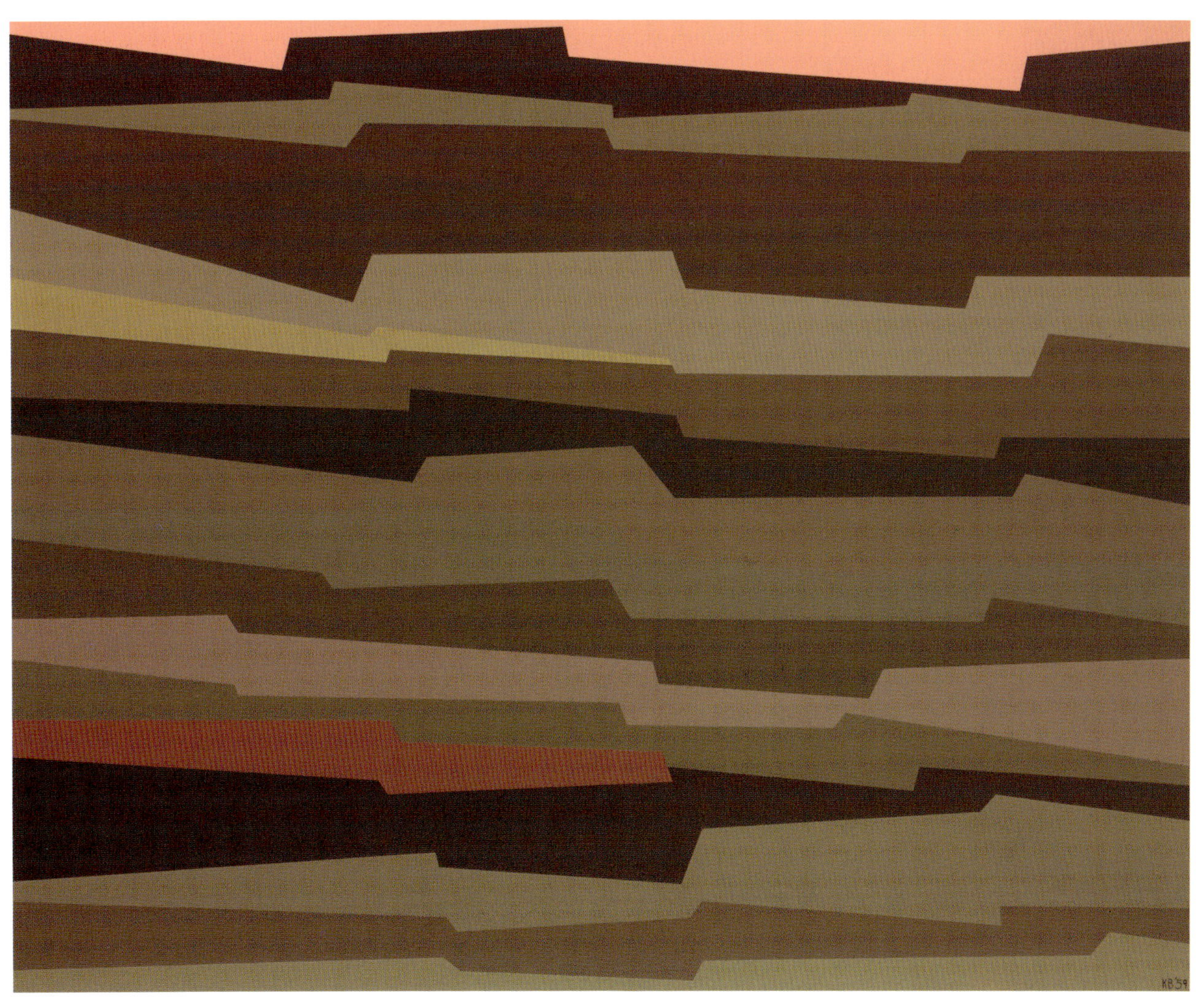

5 **vertical stripes #3**

1959
oil on canvas
42 x 48 inches
106.7 x 121.9 centimeters

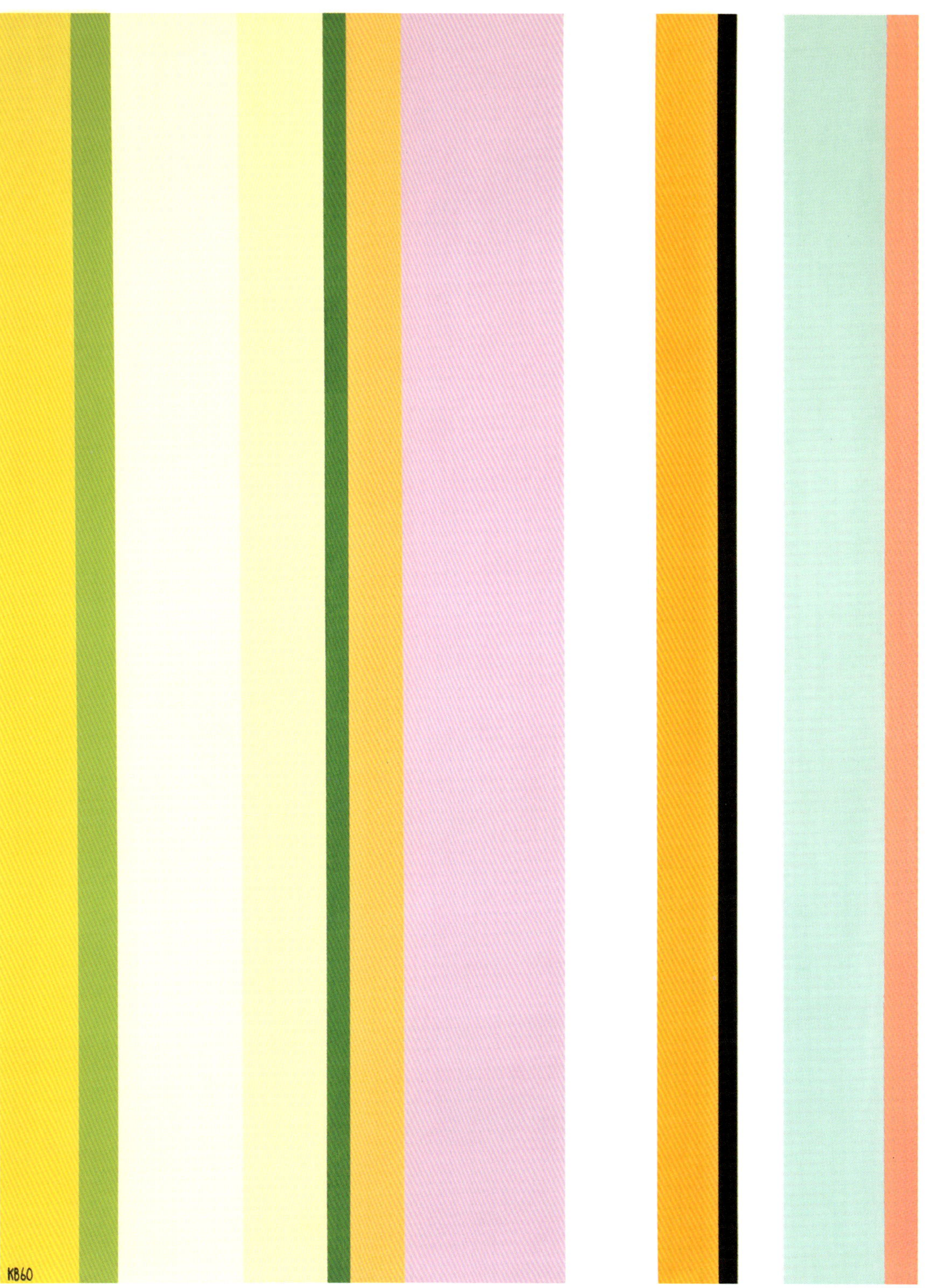
KB60

6 **vertical stripes #9**

1960
oil on canvas
40 x 30 inches
101.6 x 76.2 centimeters

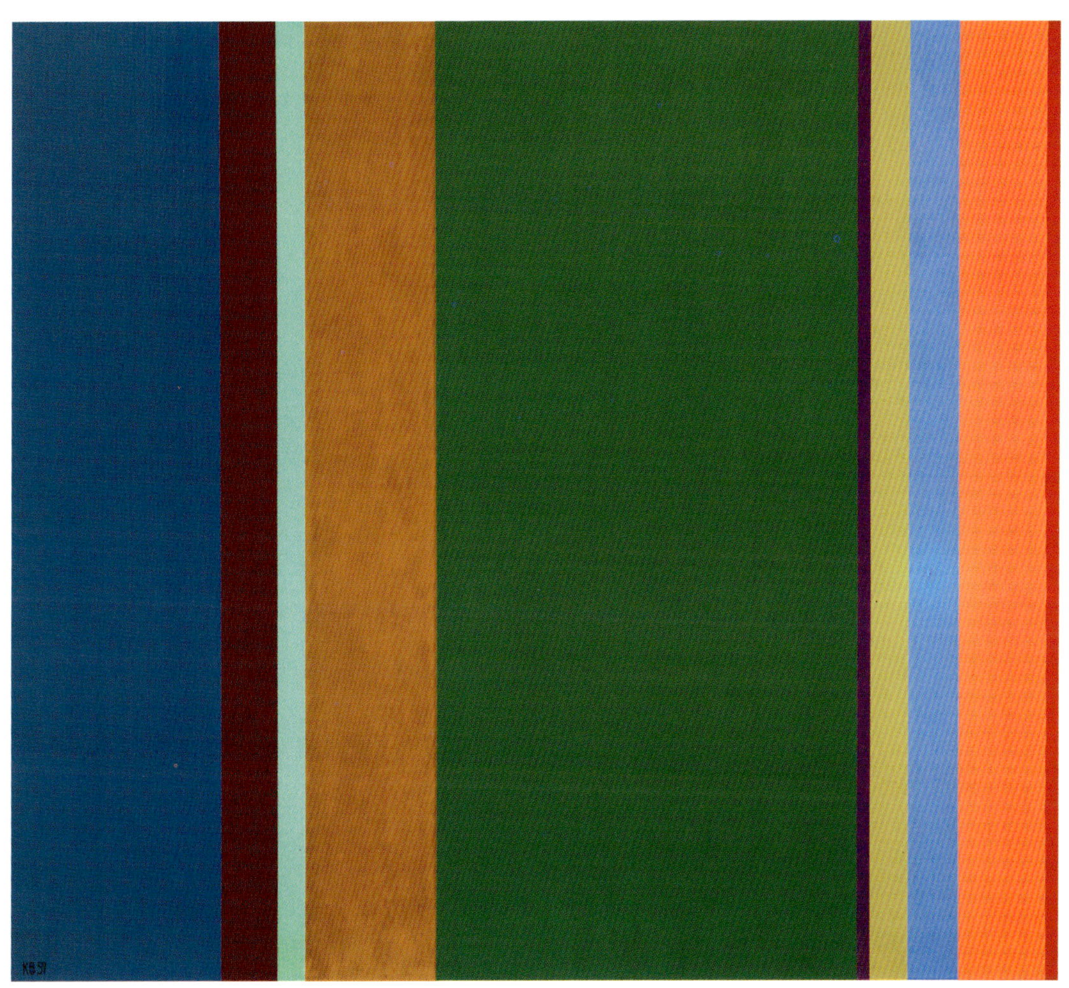

7 **black & gray**

1960
oil on canvas
28 x 36 inches
71.1 x 91.4 centimeters

8 **tape grid #3**

1960
oil on canvas
20 x 24 inches
50.8 x 61 centimeters

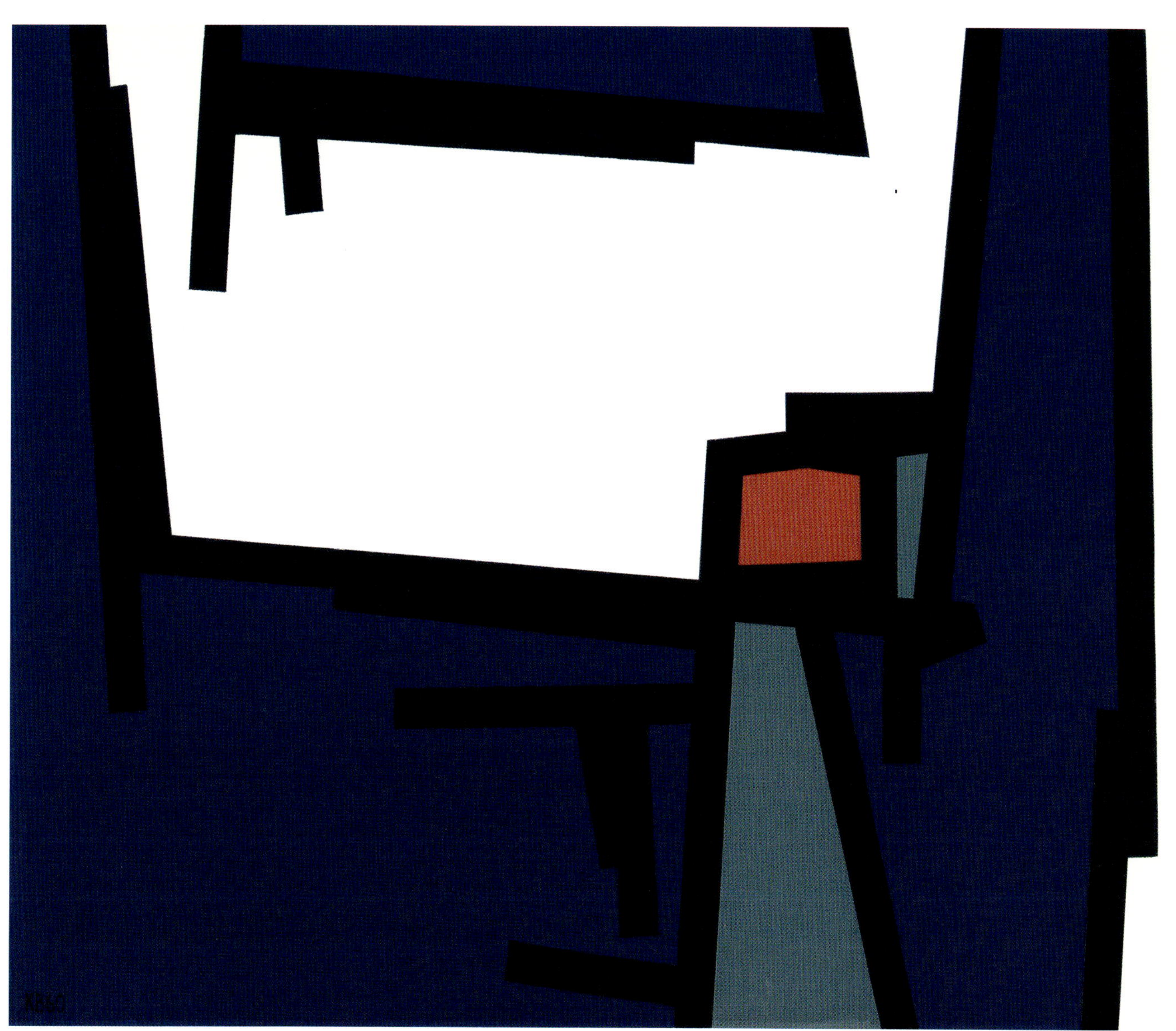

9 **tape grid #36**

1961
oil on canvas
25 x 12 1/2 inches
63.5 x 31.8 centimeters

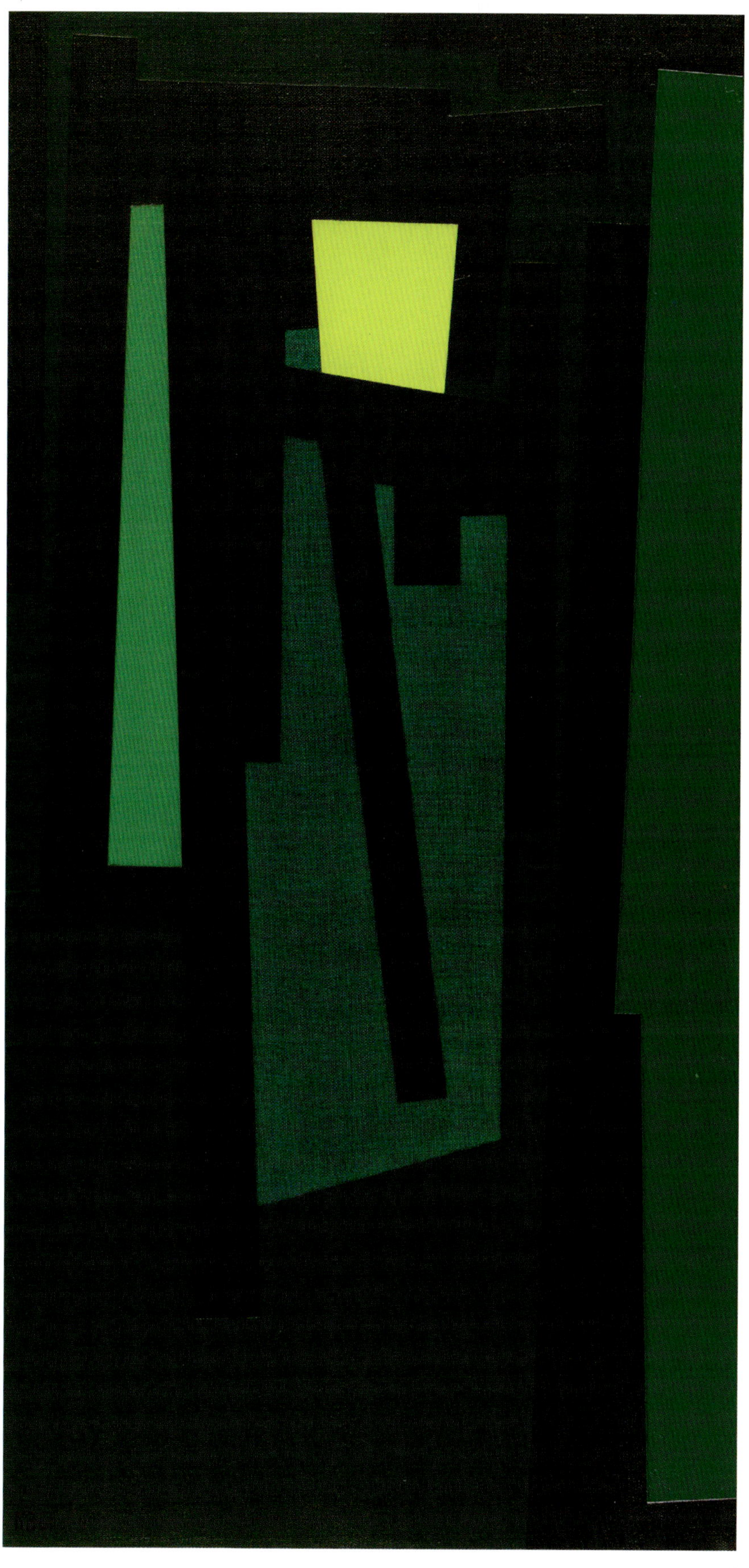

10 **floating structures #5**

1962
oil on canvas
32 x 40 inches
81.3 x 101.6 centimeters

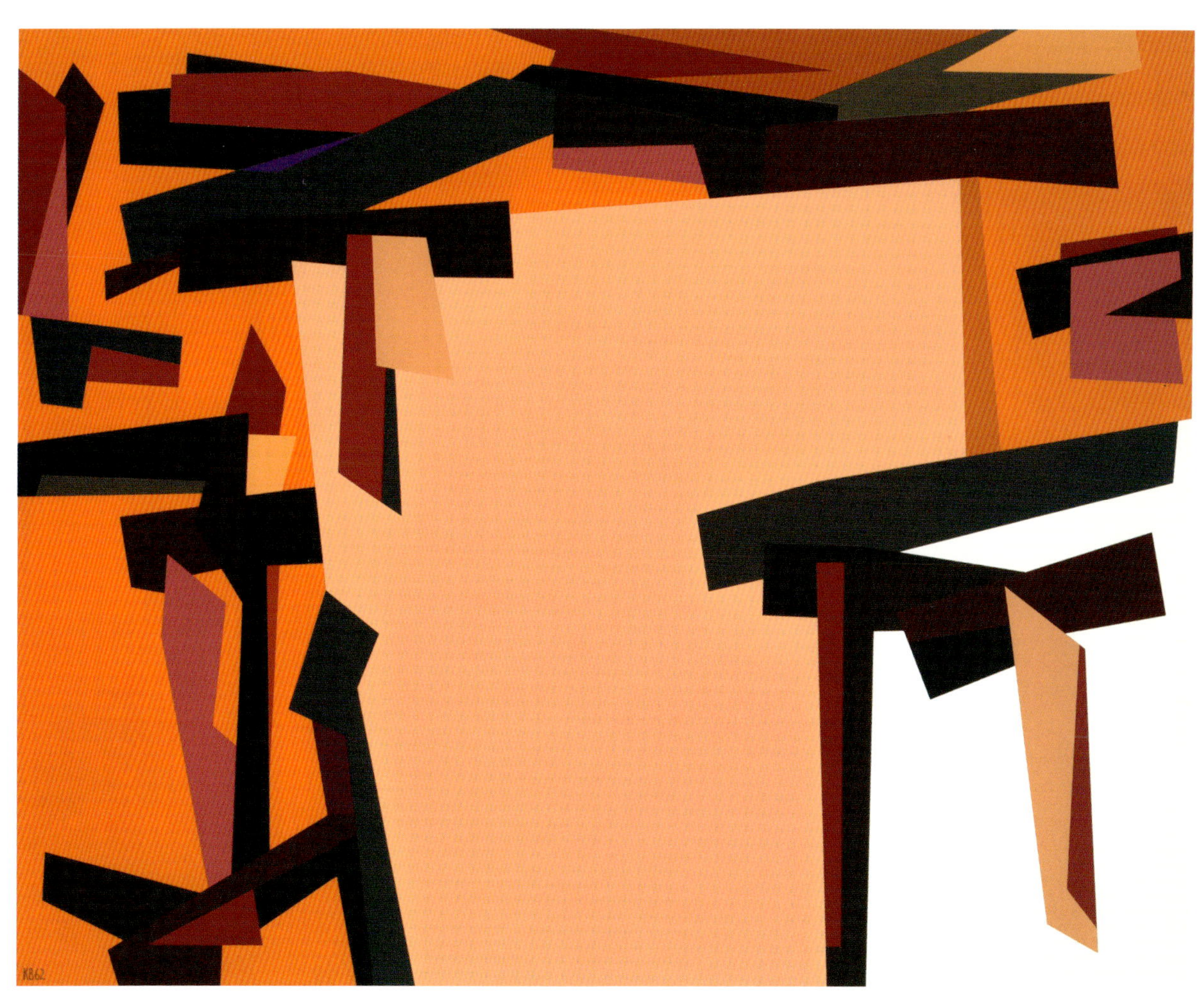

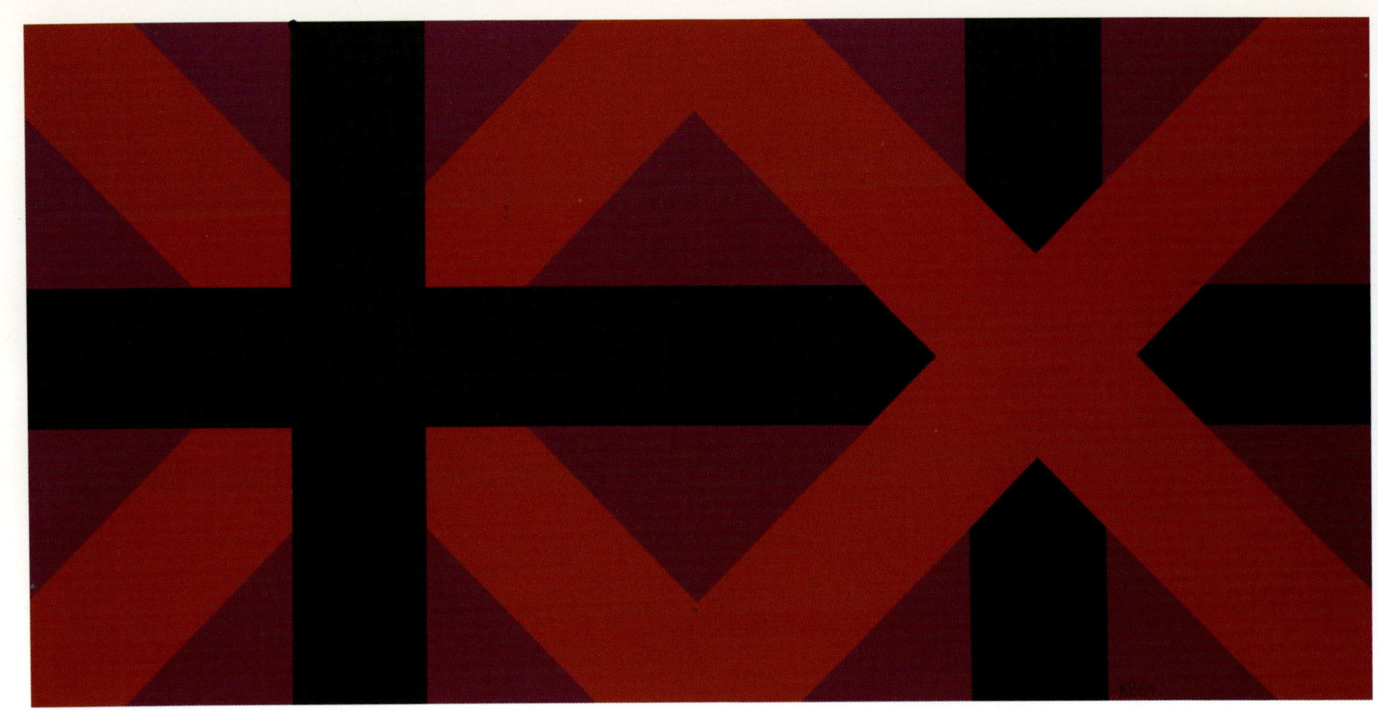

11 **#42**

1964
oil on canvas
25 1/2 x 51 inches
64.8 x 129.5 centimeters

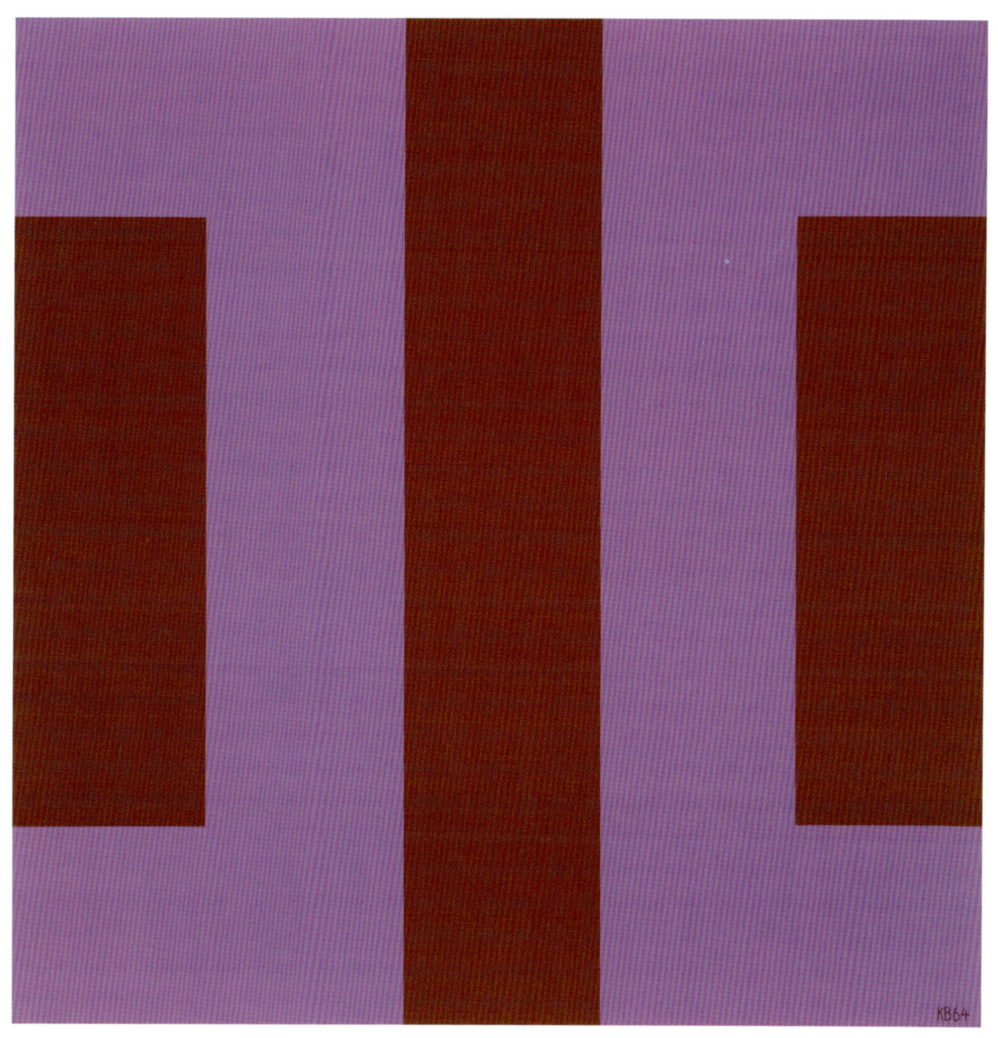

12 **#34**

1964
oil on canvas
42 x 42 inches
106.7 x 106.7 centimeters

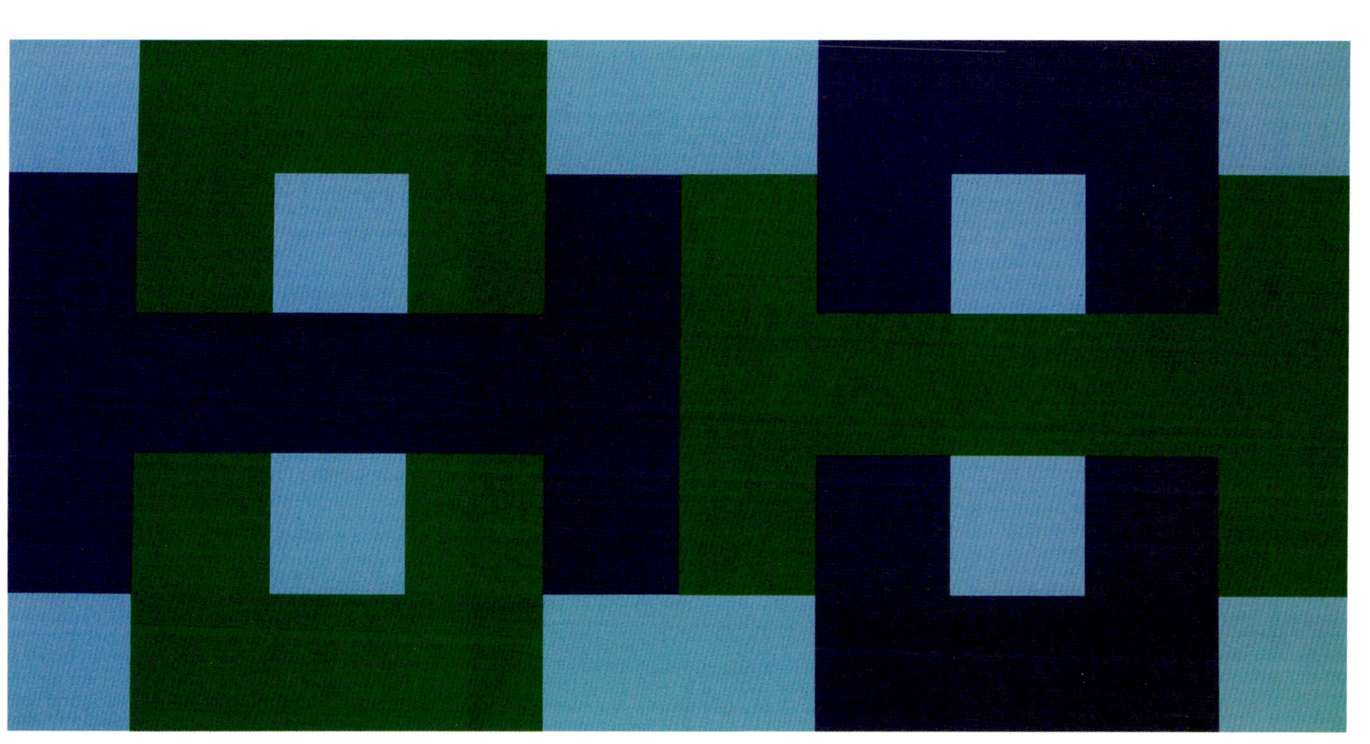

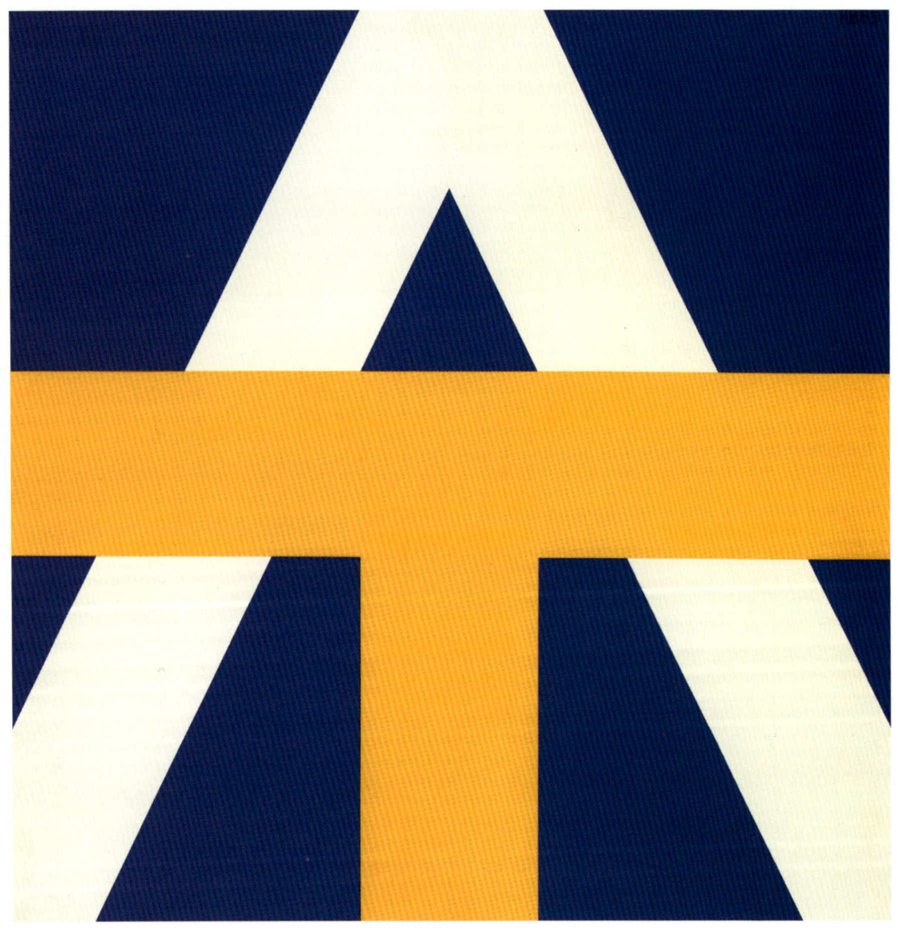

14 **#1**

1965
oil on canvas
30 x 30 inches
76.2 x 76.2 centimeters

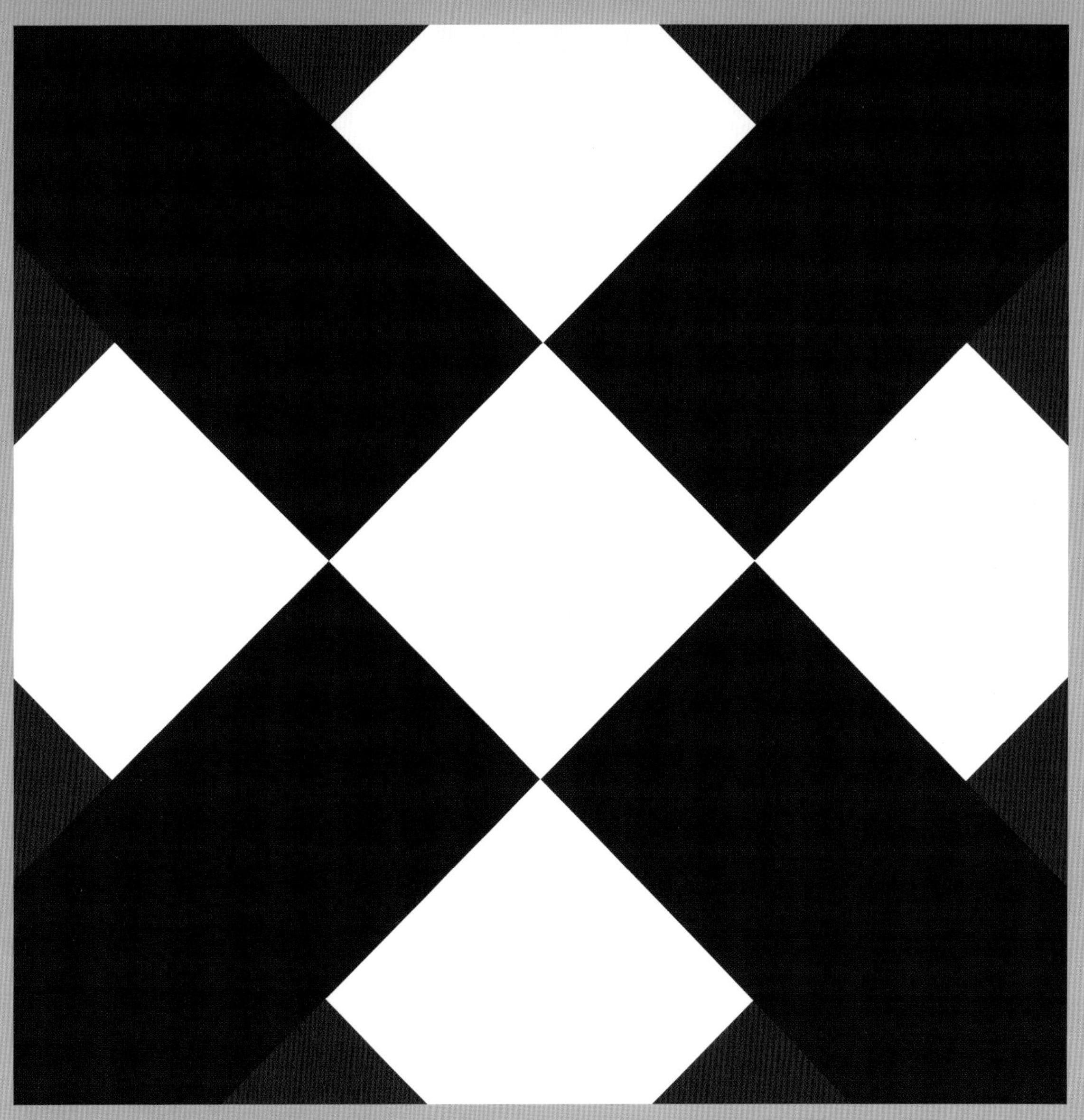

15 **#24**

1965
oil on canvas
42 x 42 inches
106.7 x 106.7 centimeters

16 **#7**

1966
oil on canvas
40 x 60 inches
101.6 x 152.4 centimeters

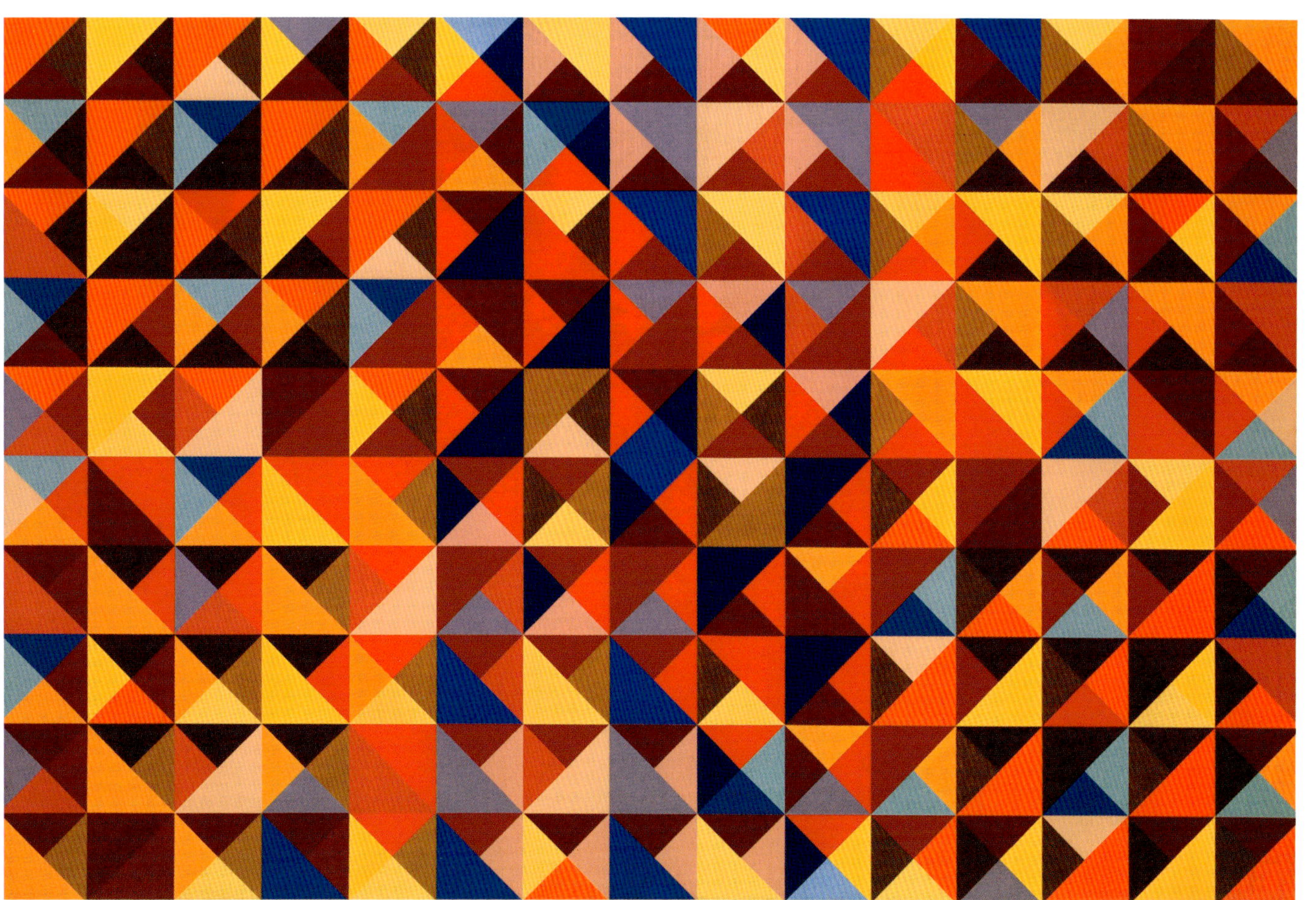

17 **#9**

1966
oil on canvas
26 x 51 inches
66 x 129.5 centimeters

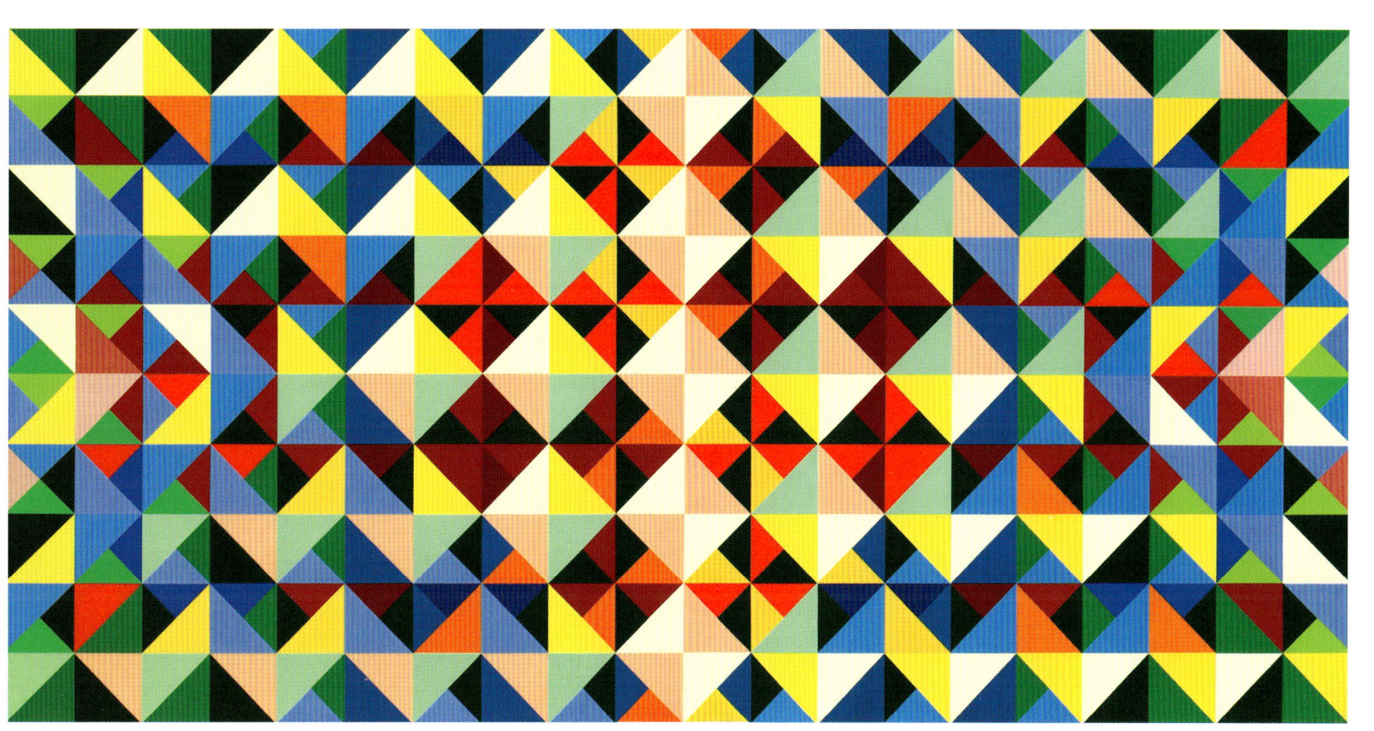

18 **#17**

1970
oil on canvas
56 3/4 x 56 3/4 inches
144.1 x 144.1 centimeters

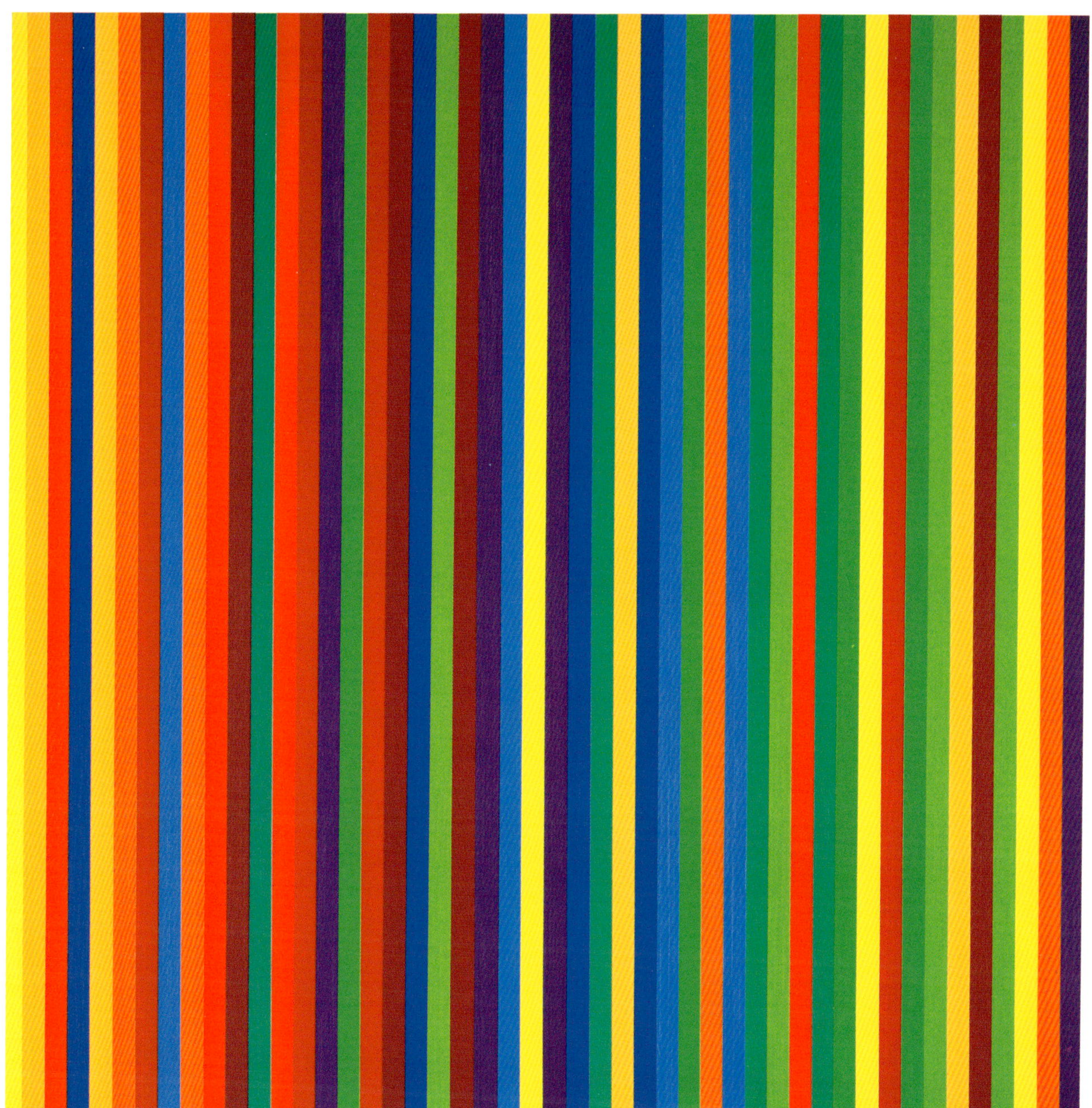

19 **#7**

1971
oil on canvas
42 x 42 inches
106.7 x 106.7 centimeters

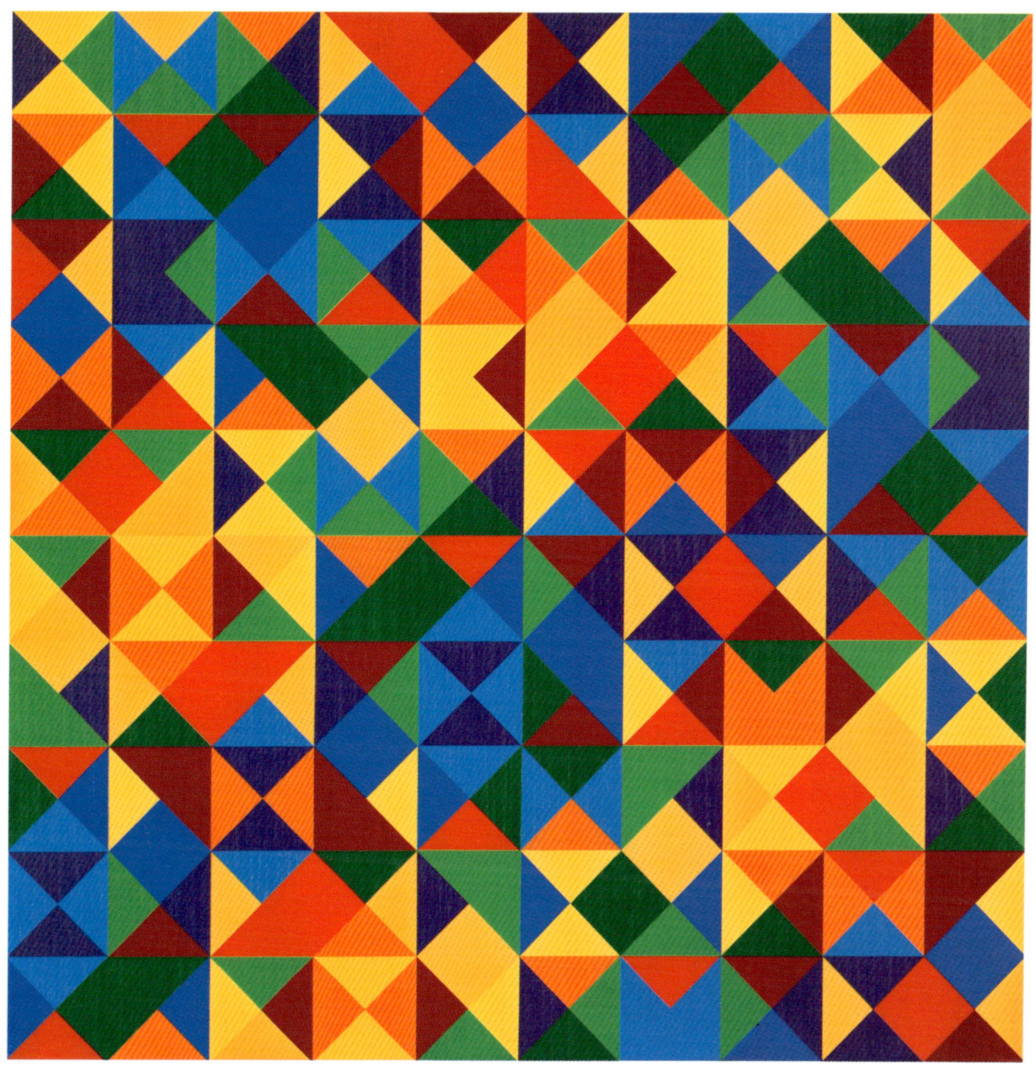

20 **#7**

1972
oil on canvas
30 x 40 inches
76.2 x 101.6 centimeters

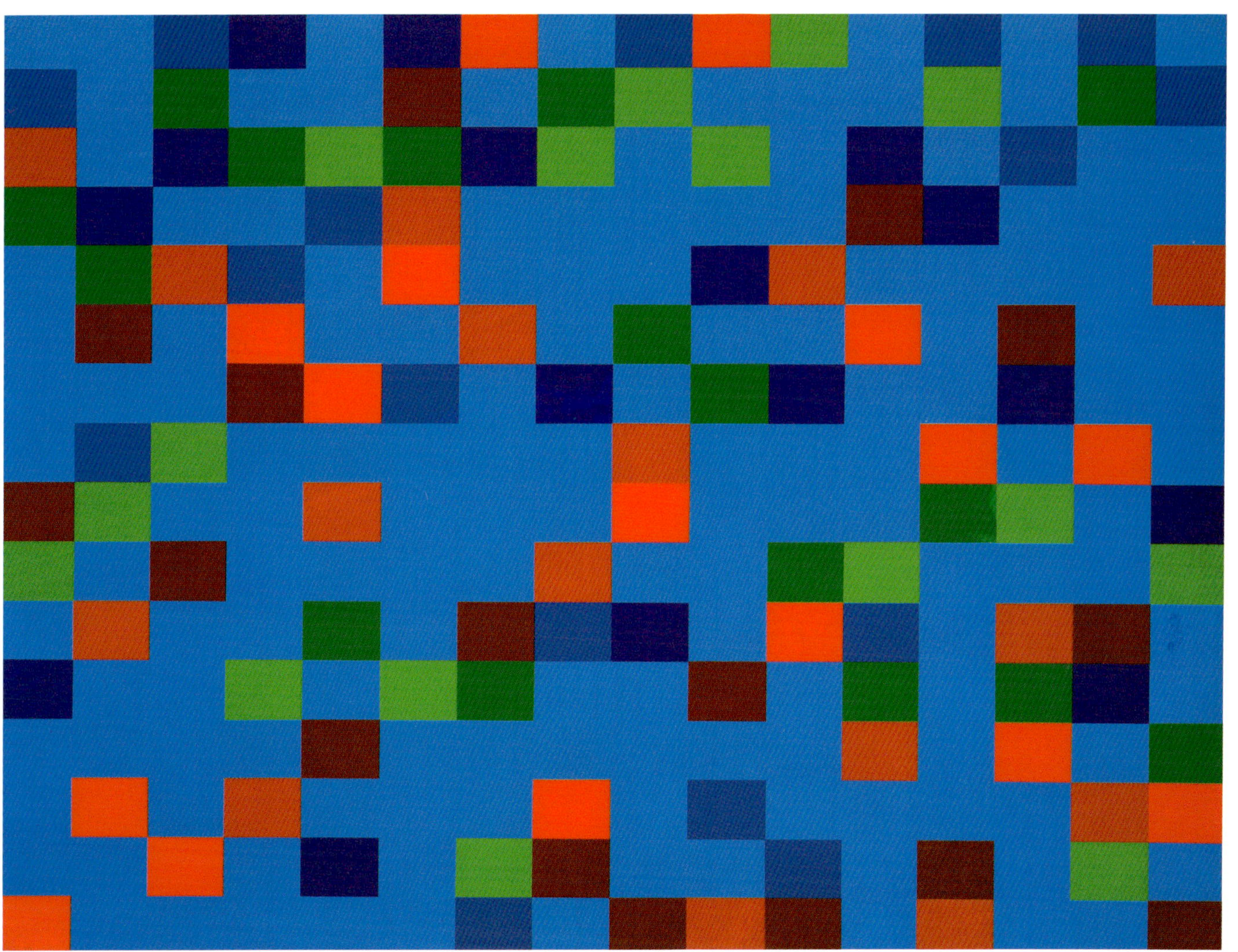

21 **#8**

1972
oil on canvas
48 x 64 inches
121.9 x 162.6 centimeters

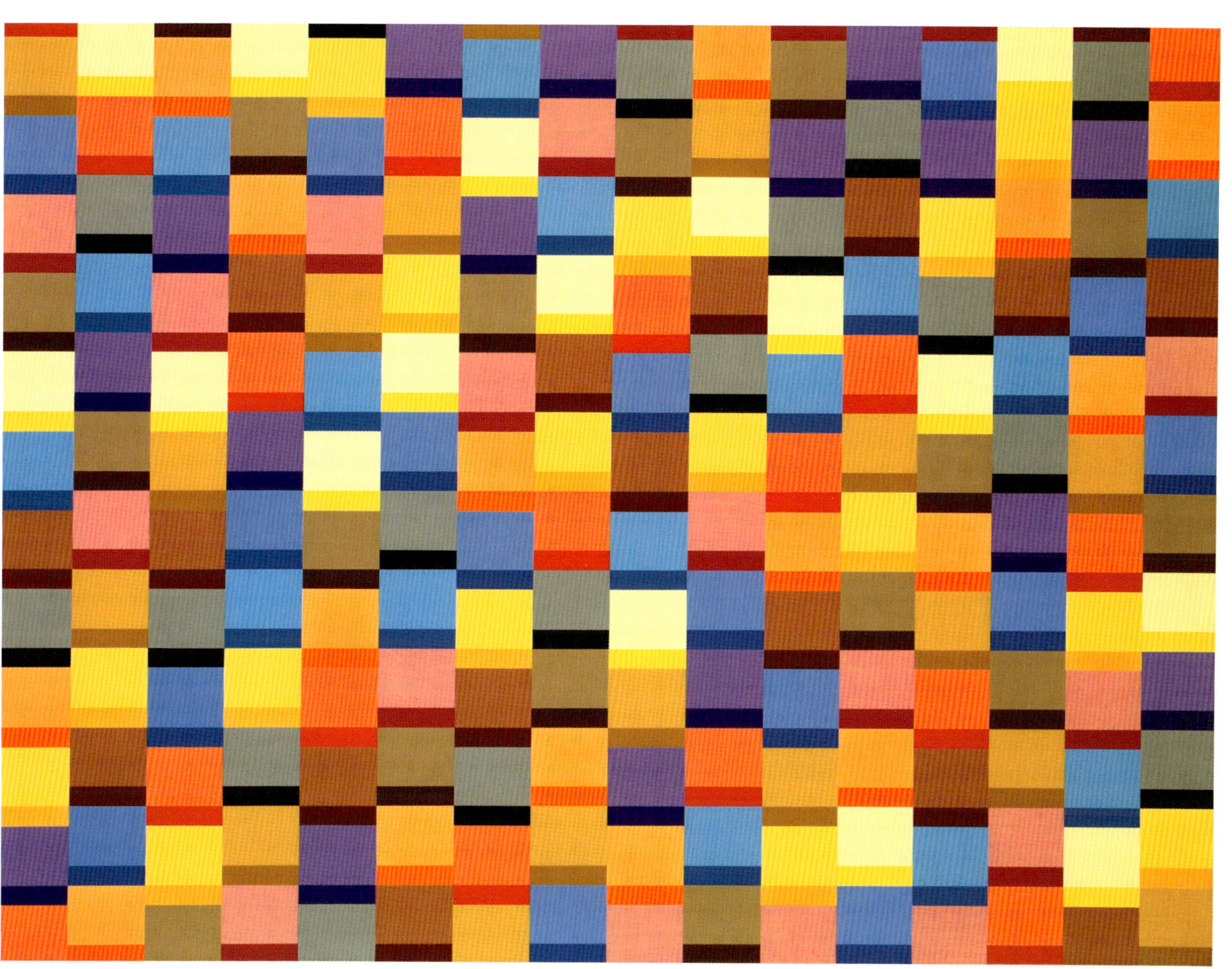

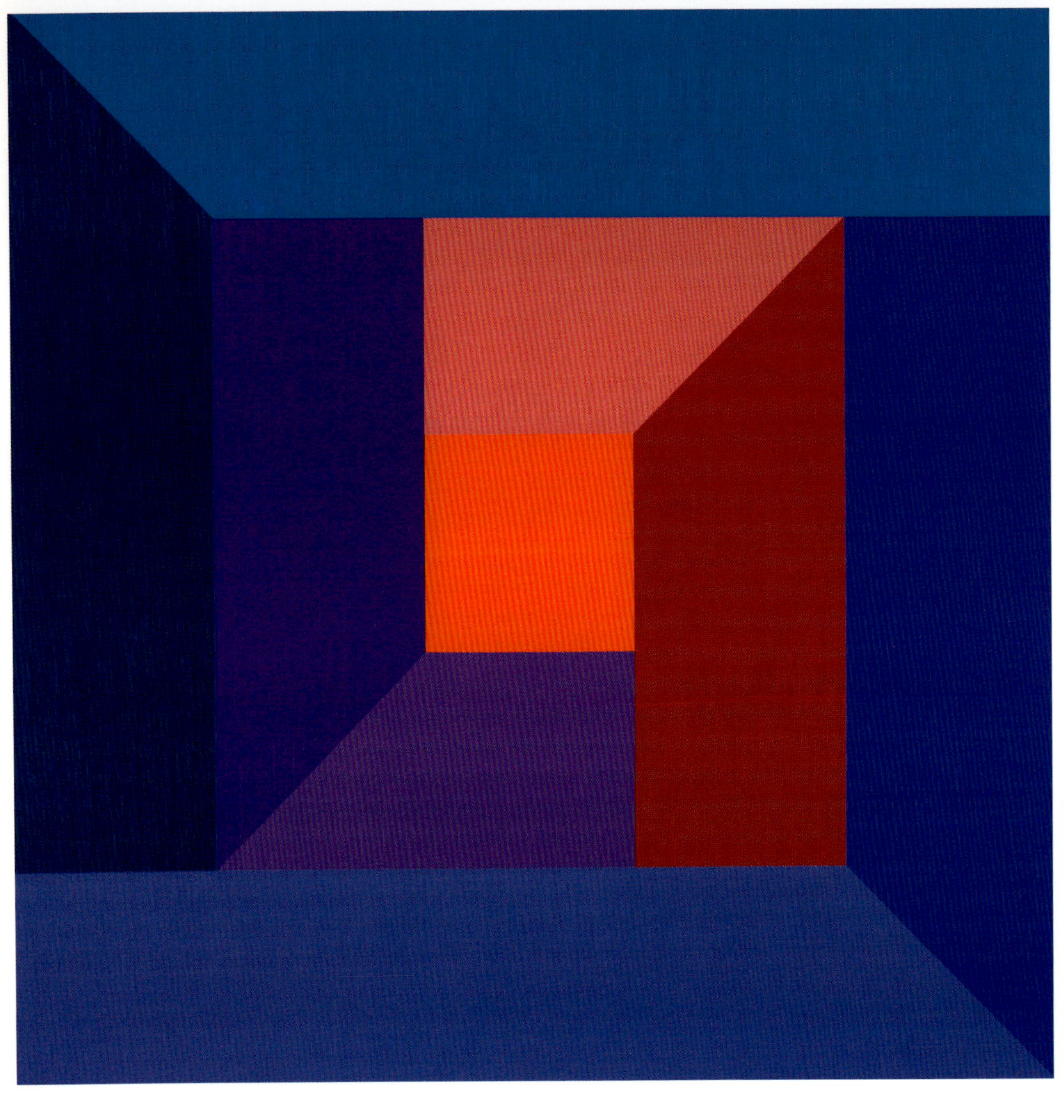

22 **#7**

1974
oil on canvas
40 x 40 inches
101.6 x 101.6 centimeters

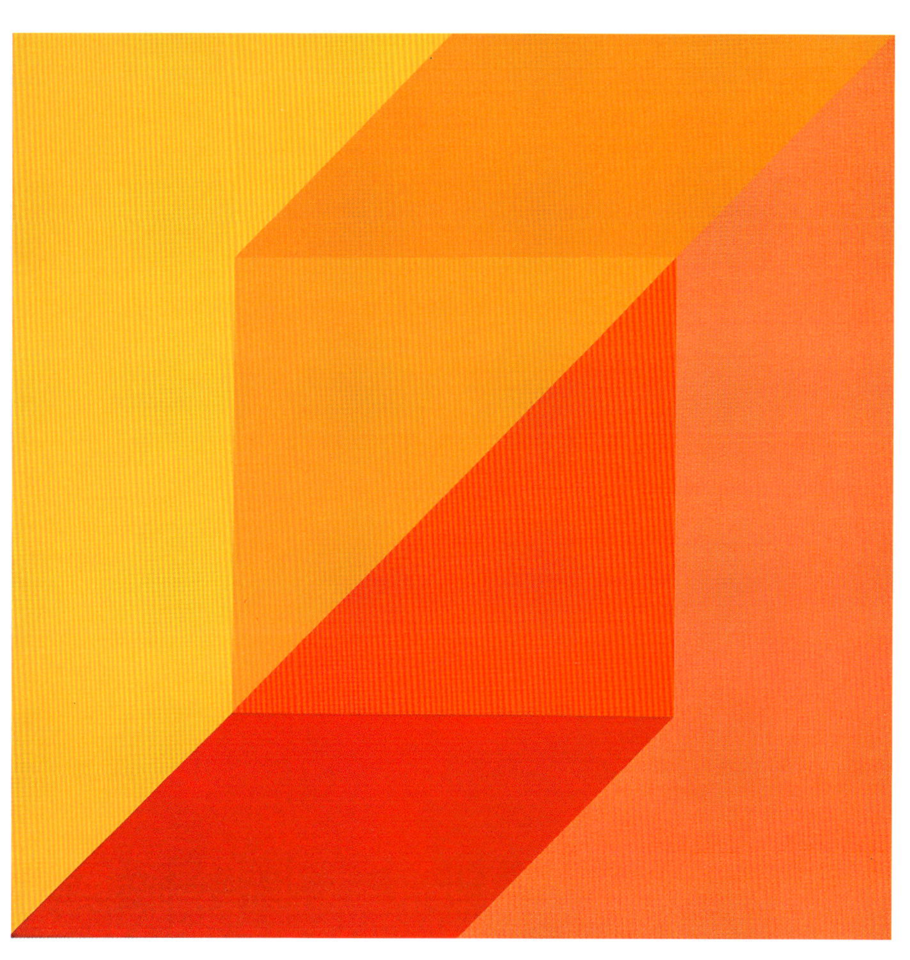

23 **#11**

1975
oil on canvas
28 x 28 inches
71.1 x 71.1 centimeters

24 **#1**

1976
oil on canvas
59 1/2 x 47 1/2 inches
151.1 x 120.7 centimeters

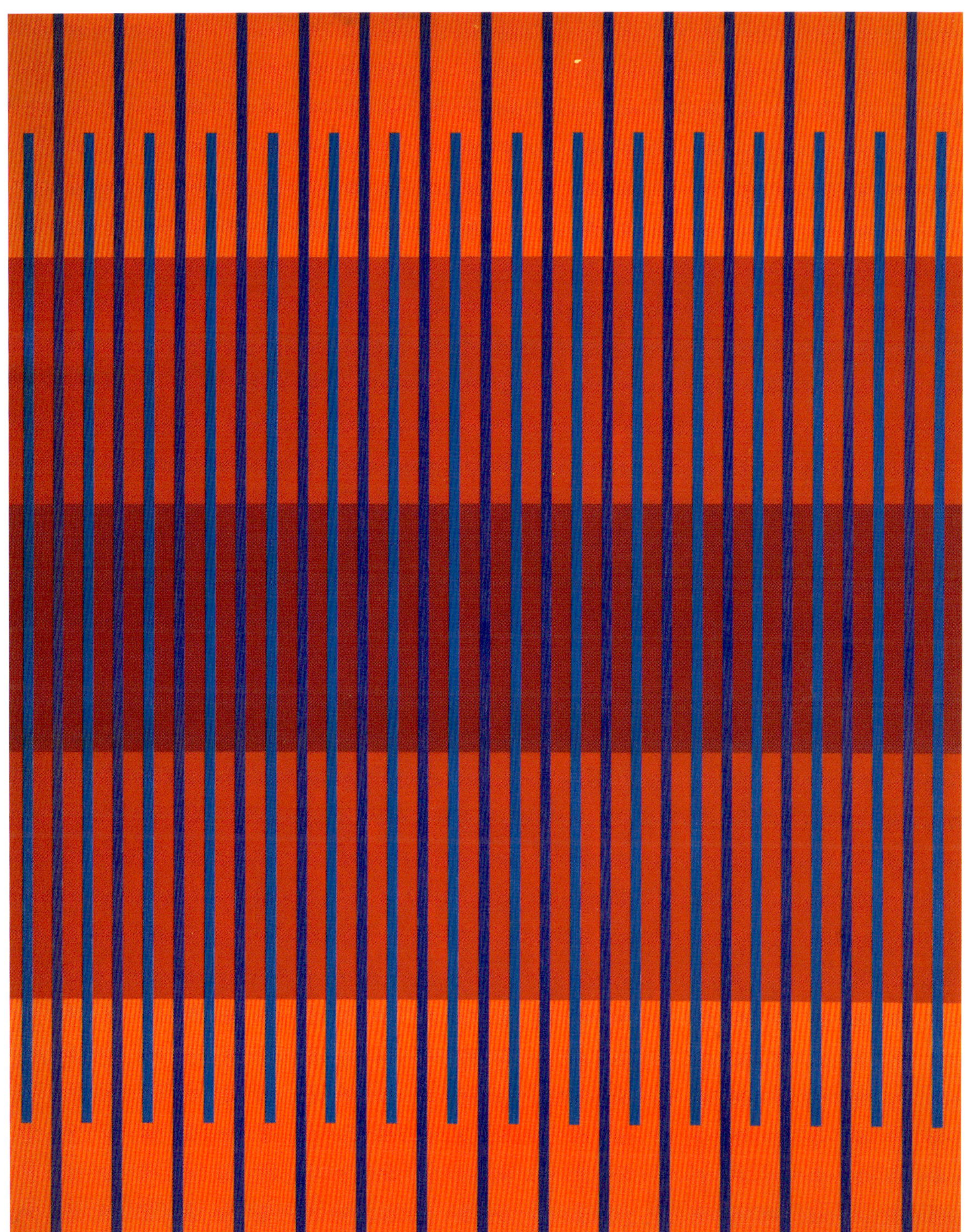

25 **#25**

1977
oil on canvas
50 x 40 1/2 inches
127 x 102.9 centimeters

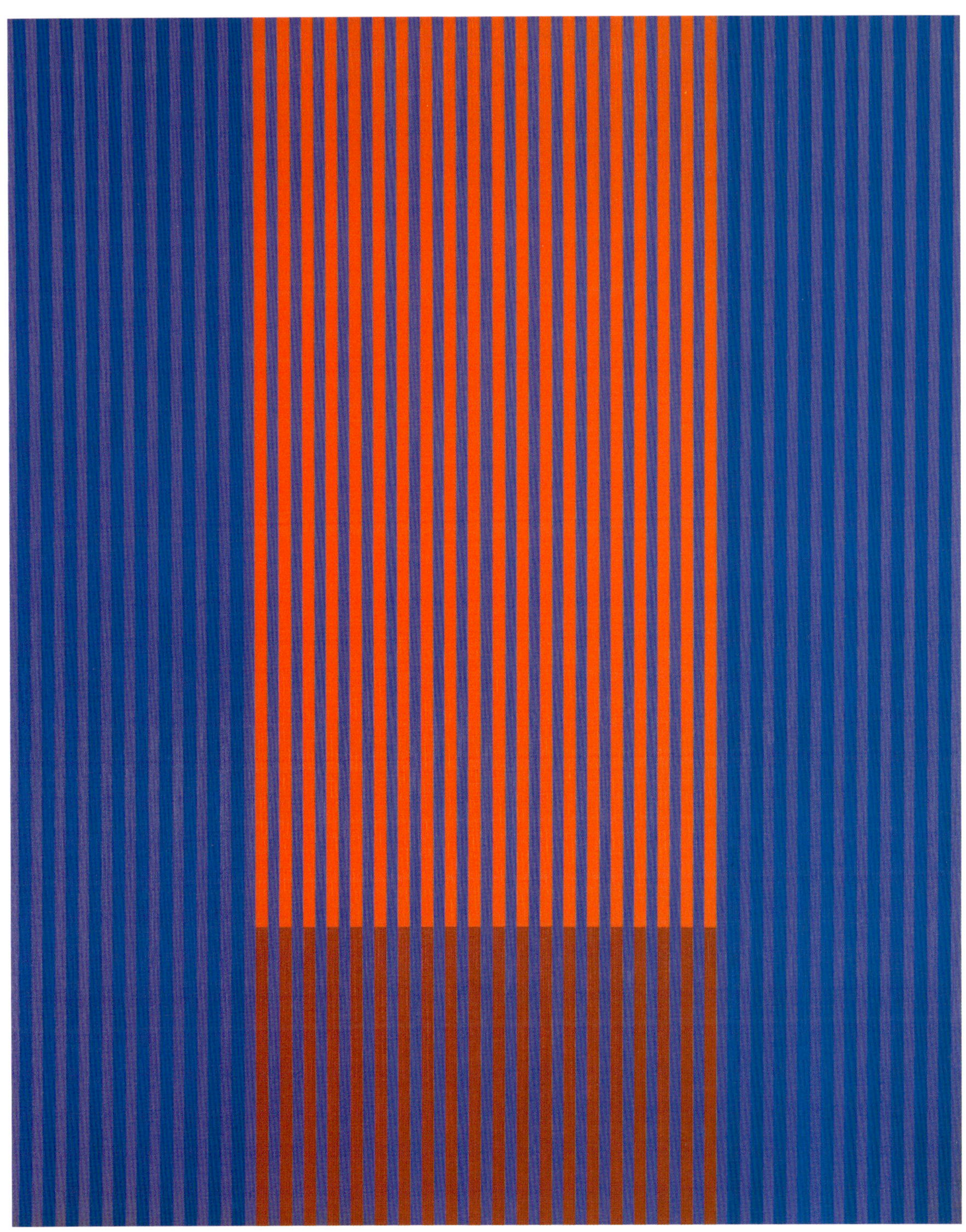

26 **#21**

1979
oil on canvas
72 x 54 inches
182.9 x 137.2 centimeters

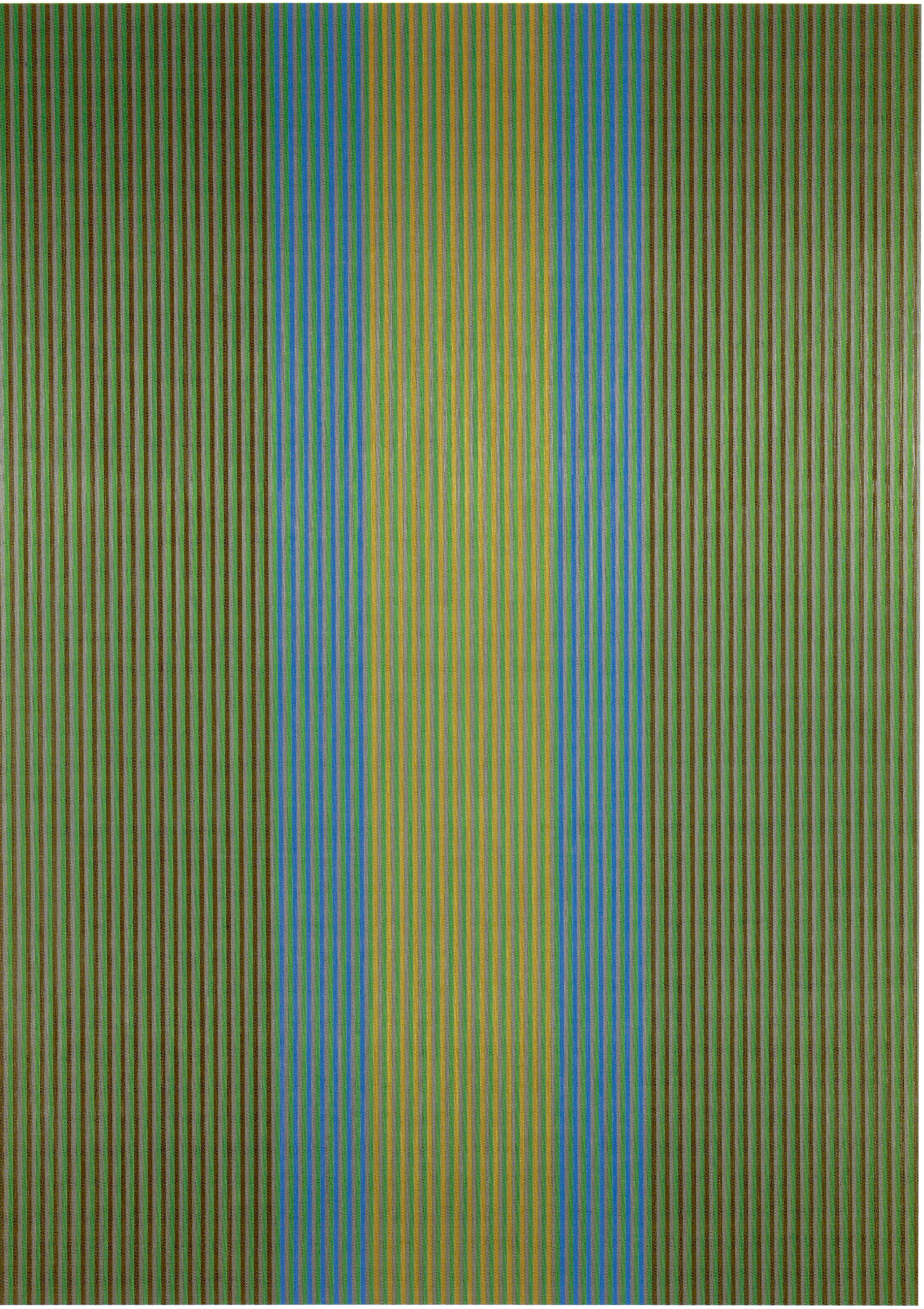

27 **#3**

1980
oil on canvas
72 x 54 inches
182.9 x 137.2 centimeters

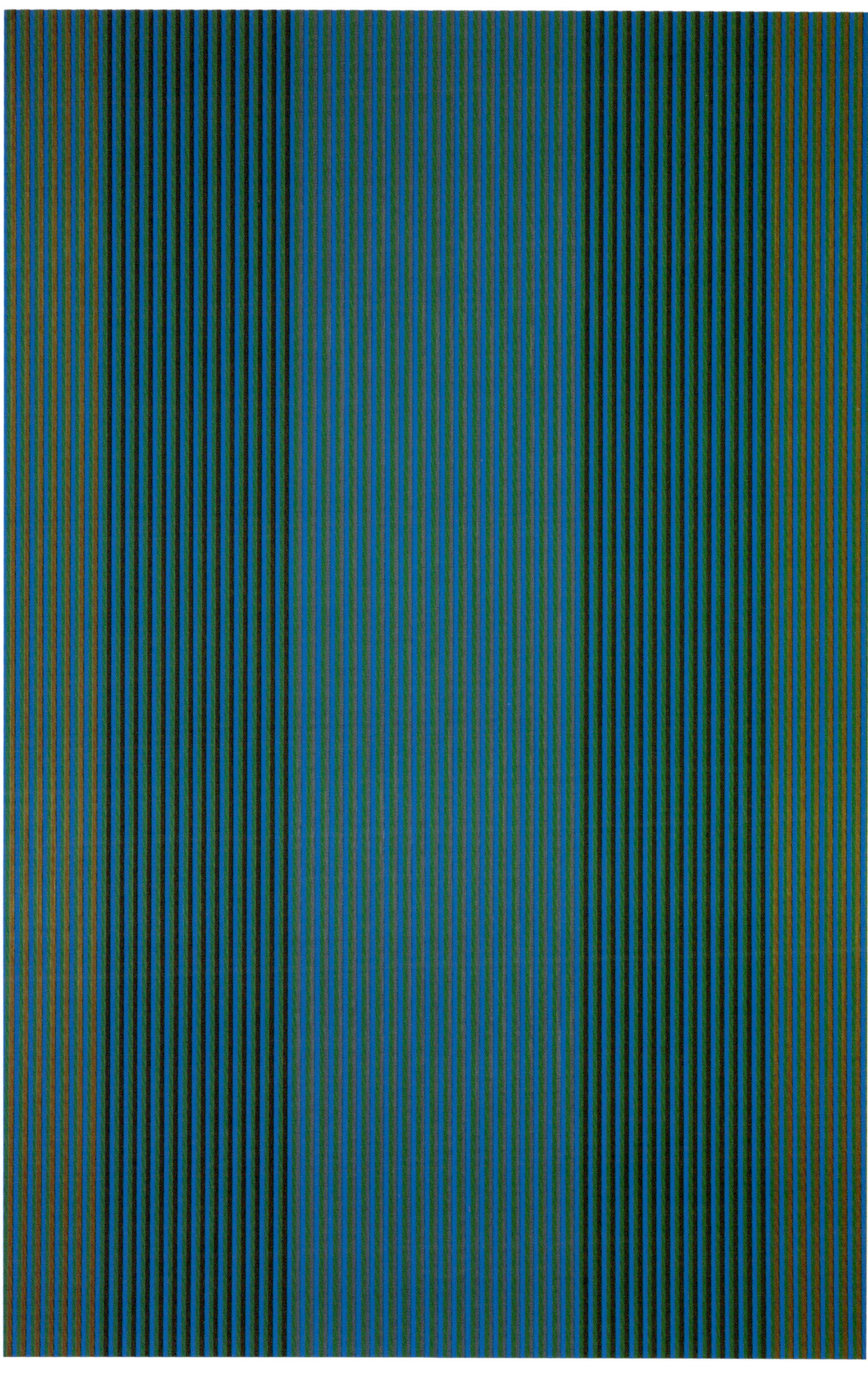

28 **#1**

1980
oil on canvas
72 x 48 inches
182.9 x 121.9 centimeters

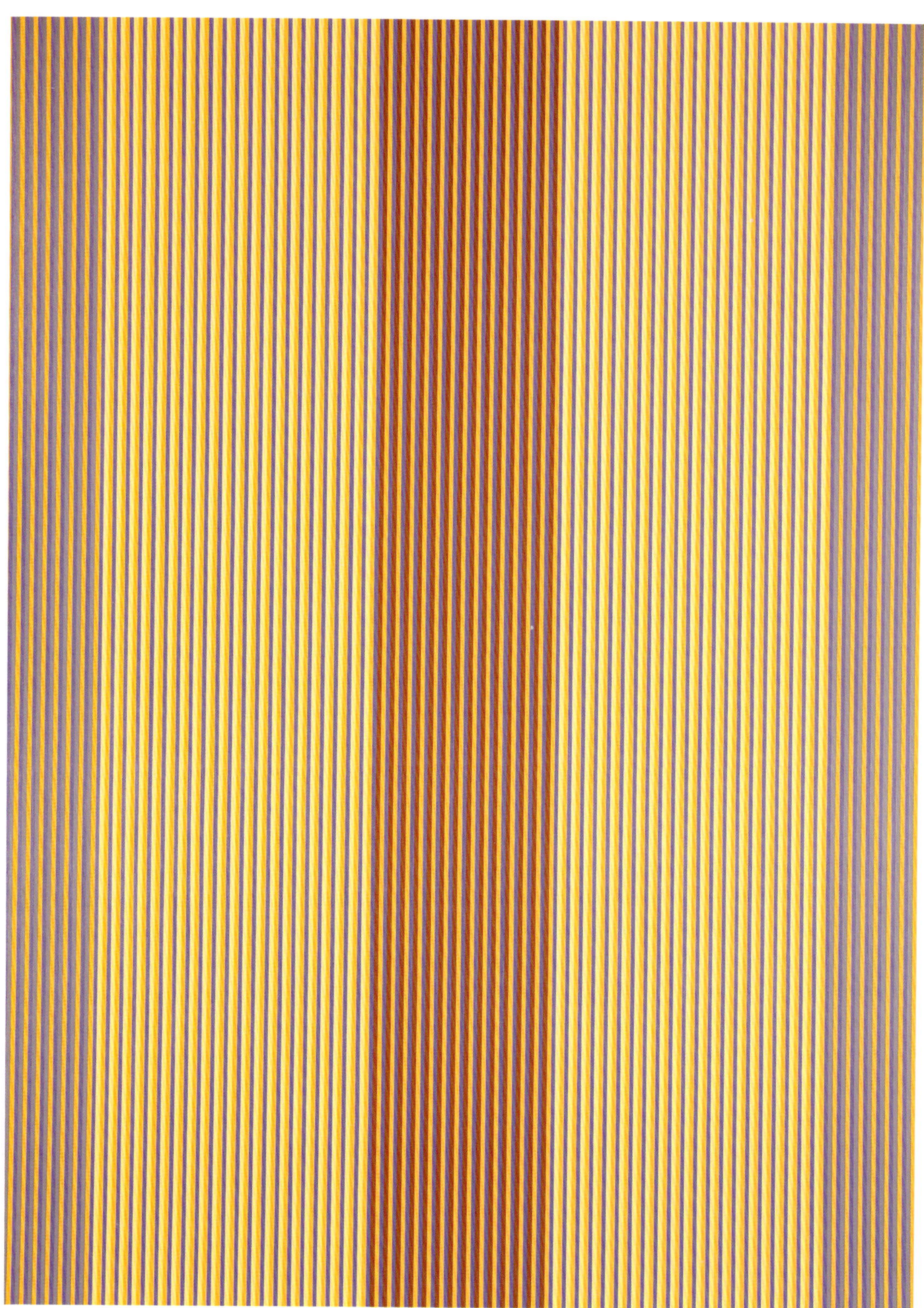

29 **#8**

1980
oil on canvas
72 x 48 inches
182.9 x 121.9 centimeters

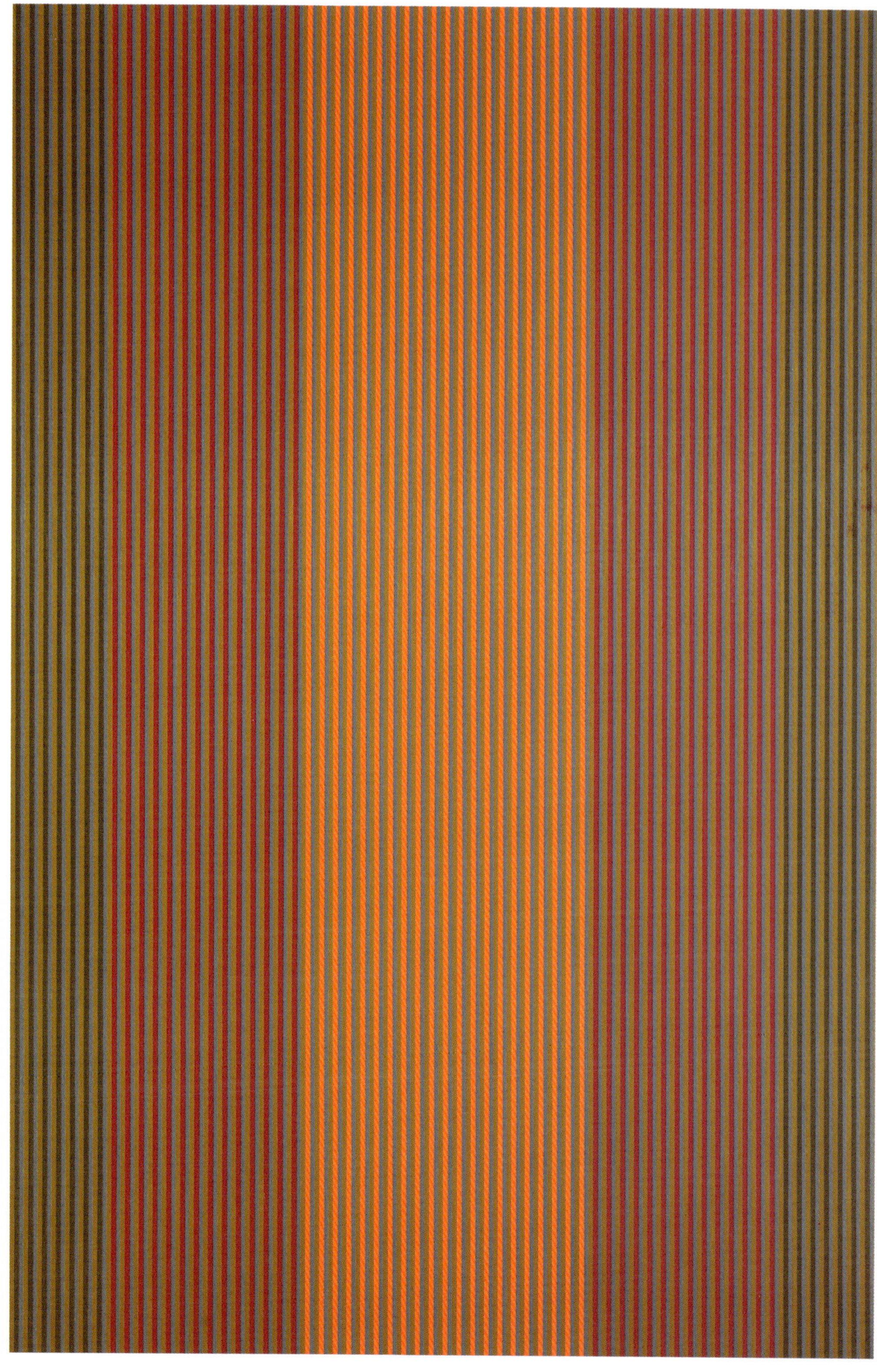

30 **#16**

1981
oil on canvas
60 x 60 inches
152.4 x 152.4 centimeters

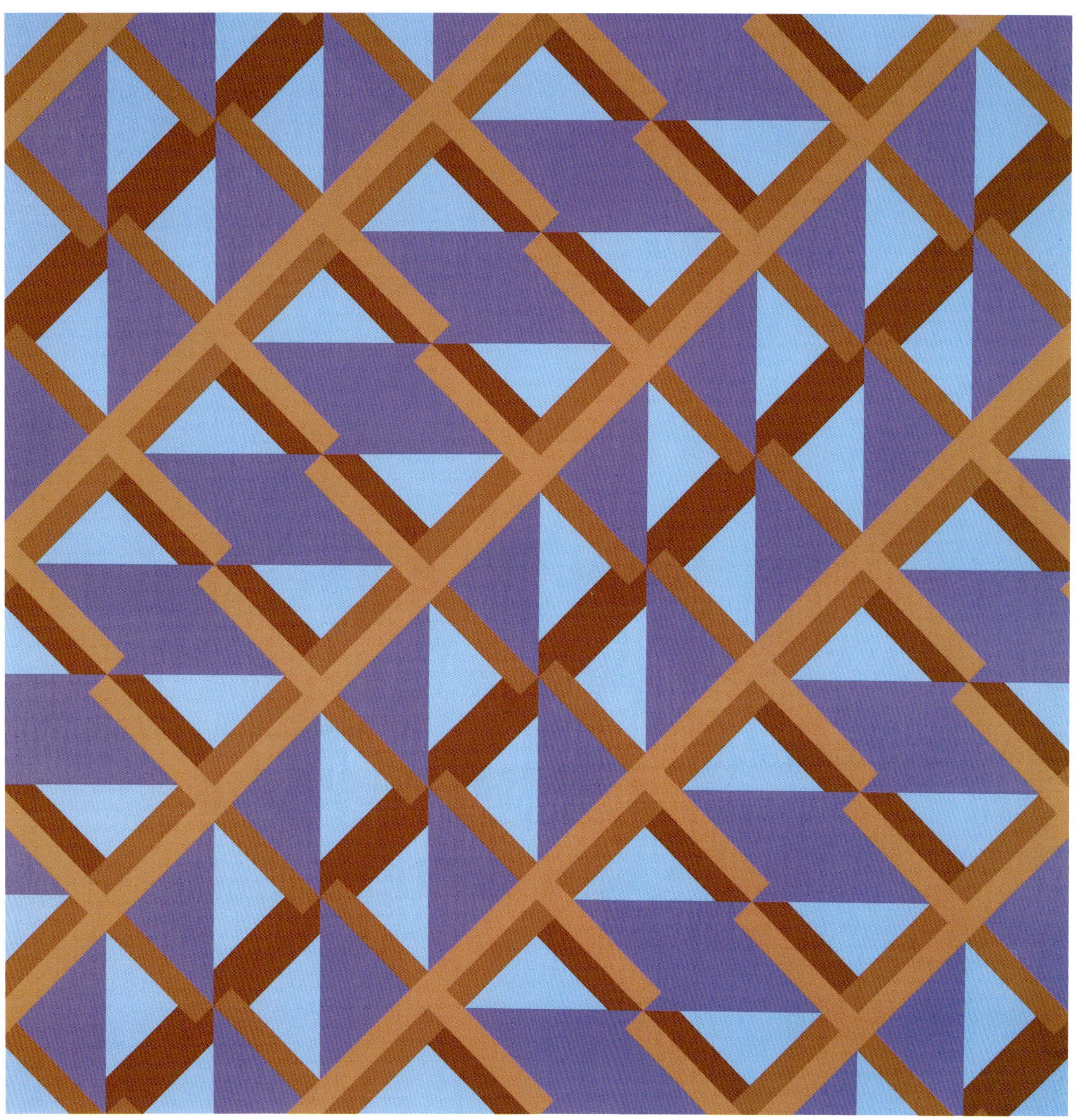

31 **#1**

1982
oil on canvas
60 x 60 inches
152.4 x 152.4 centimeters

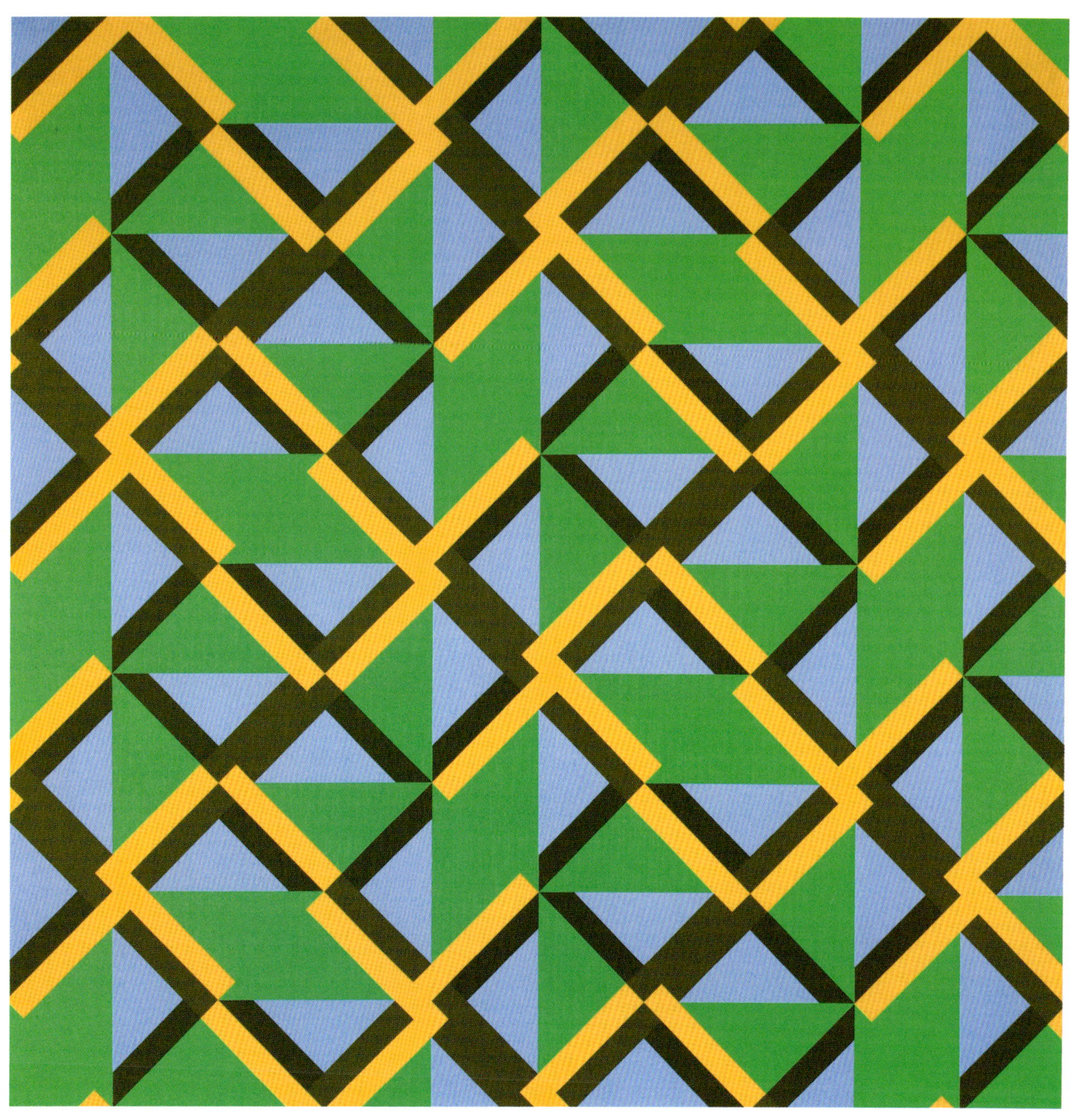

32 **#9**

1982
oil on canvas
60 x 60 inches
152.4 x 152.4 centimeters

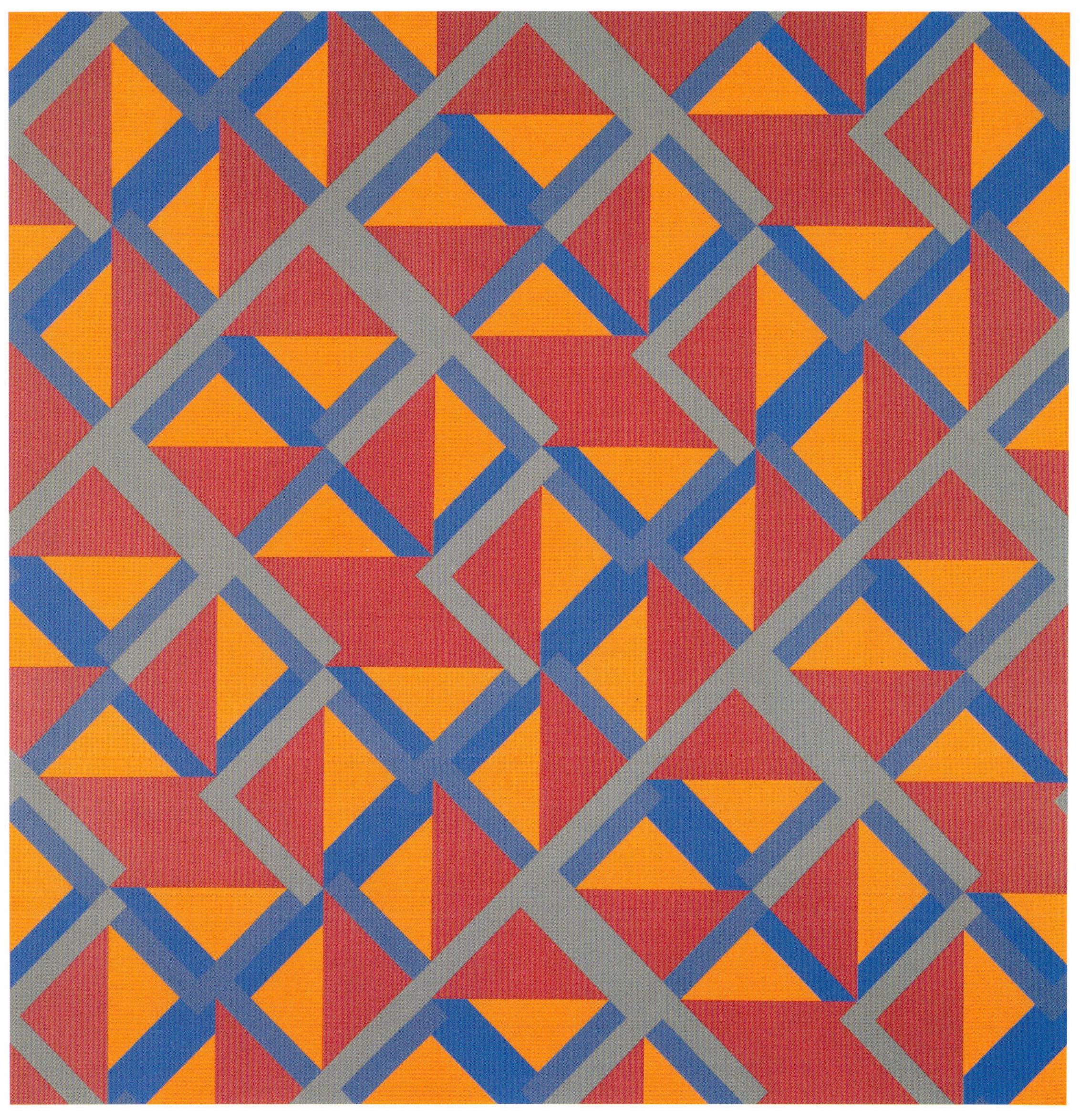

33 **#10**

1982
oil on canvas
63 x 45 inches
160 x 114.3 centimeters

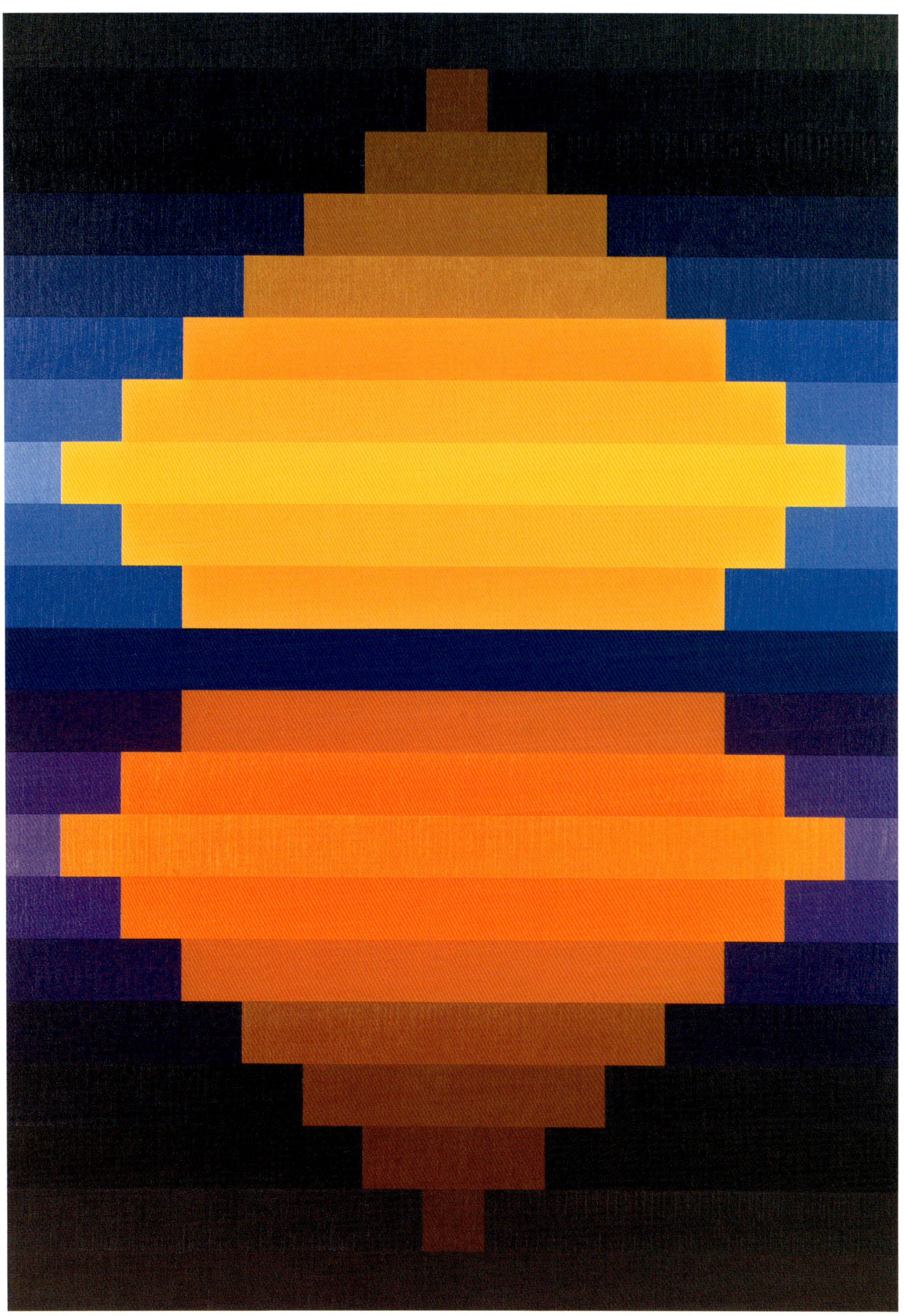

34 **#3**

1983
oil on canvas
63 x 45 inches
160 x 114.3 centimeters

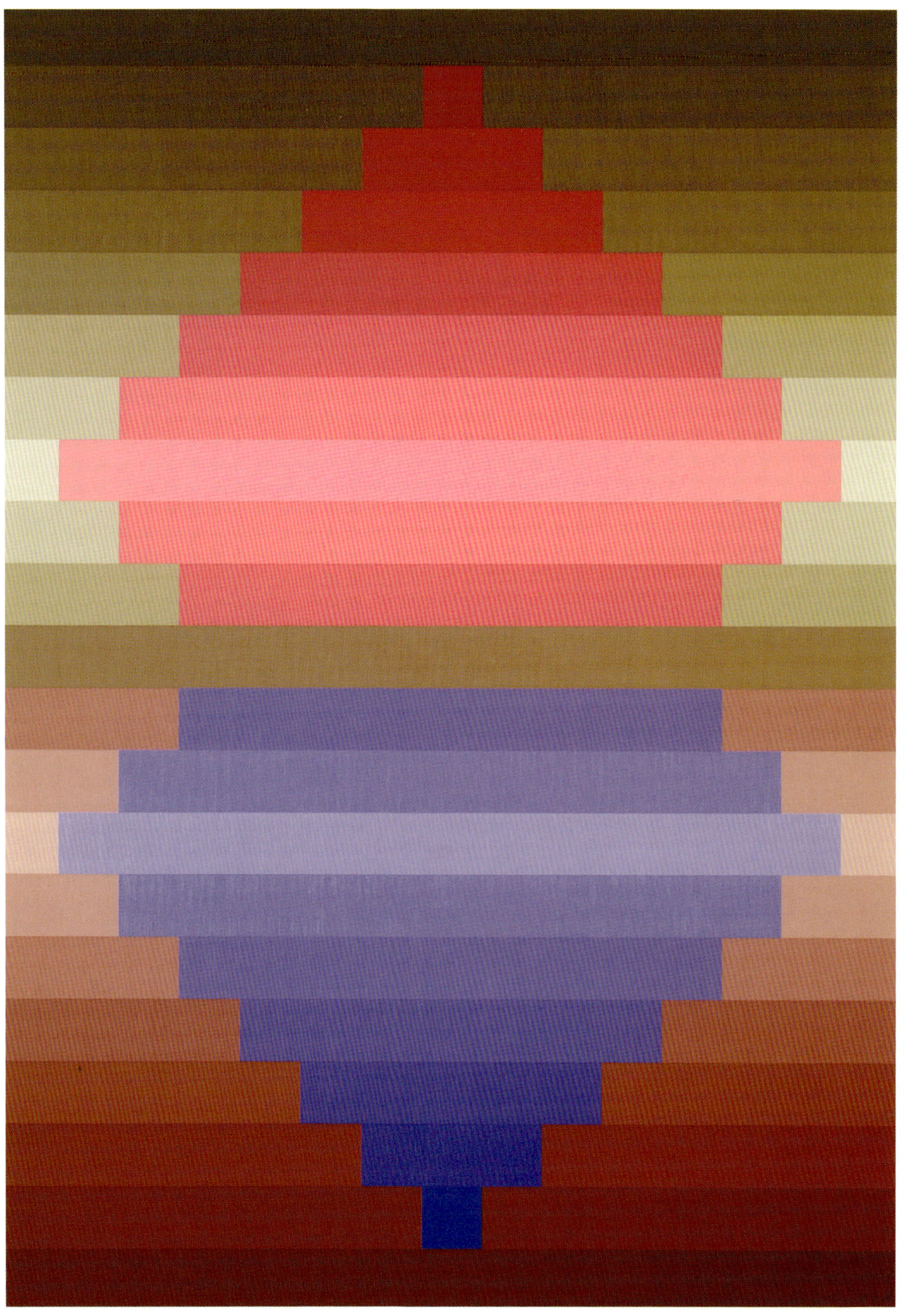

35 **#14**

1984
oil on canvas
60 x 60 inches
152.4 x 152.4 centimeters

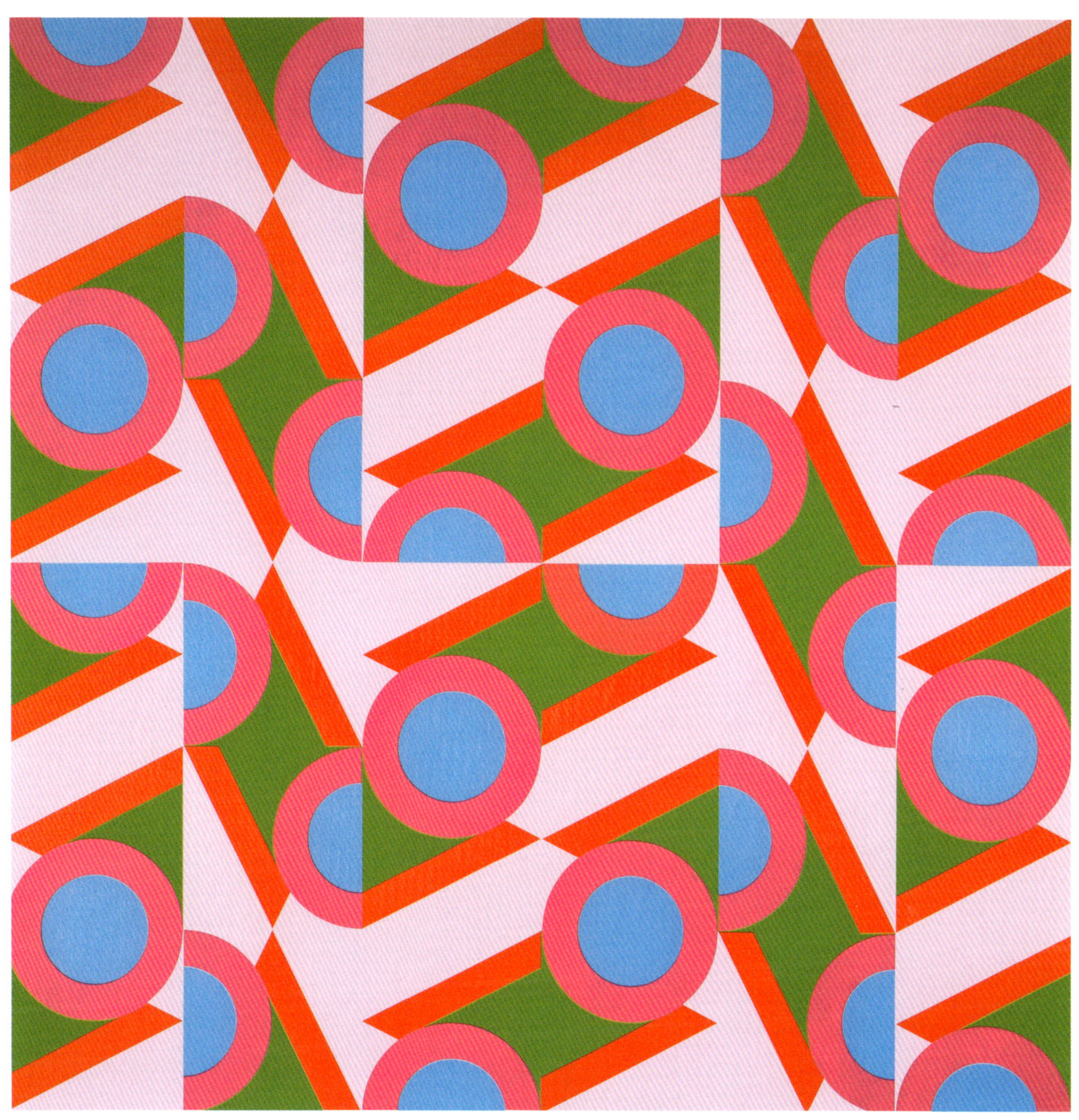

#15

1984
oil on canvas
60 x 60 inches
152.4 x 152.4 centimeters

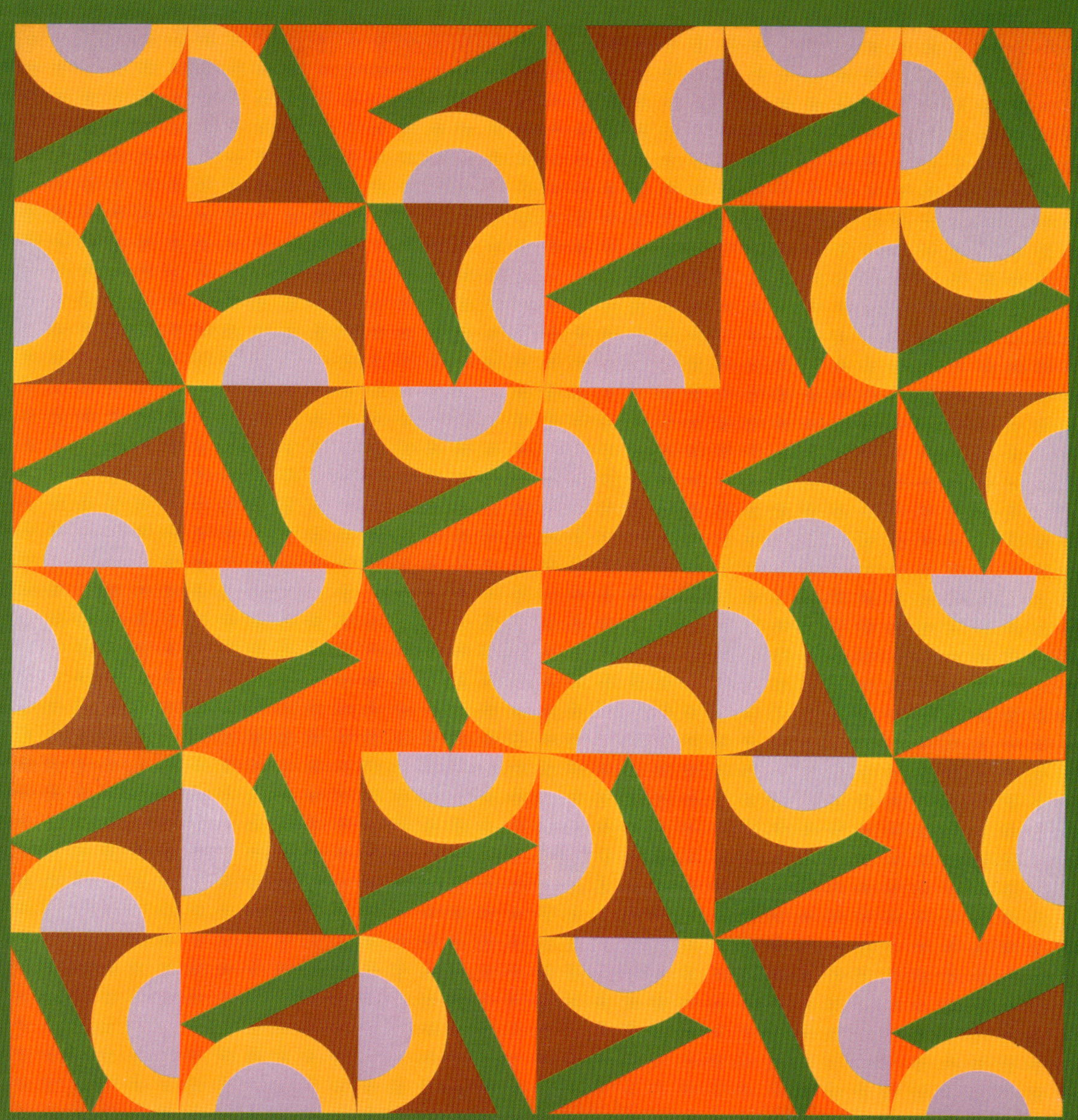

37 **#7**

1985
oil on canvas
60 x 60 inches
152.4 x 152.4 centimeters

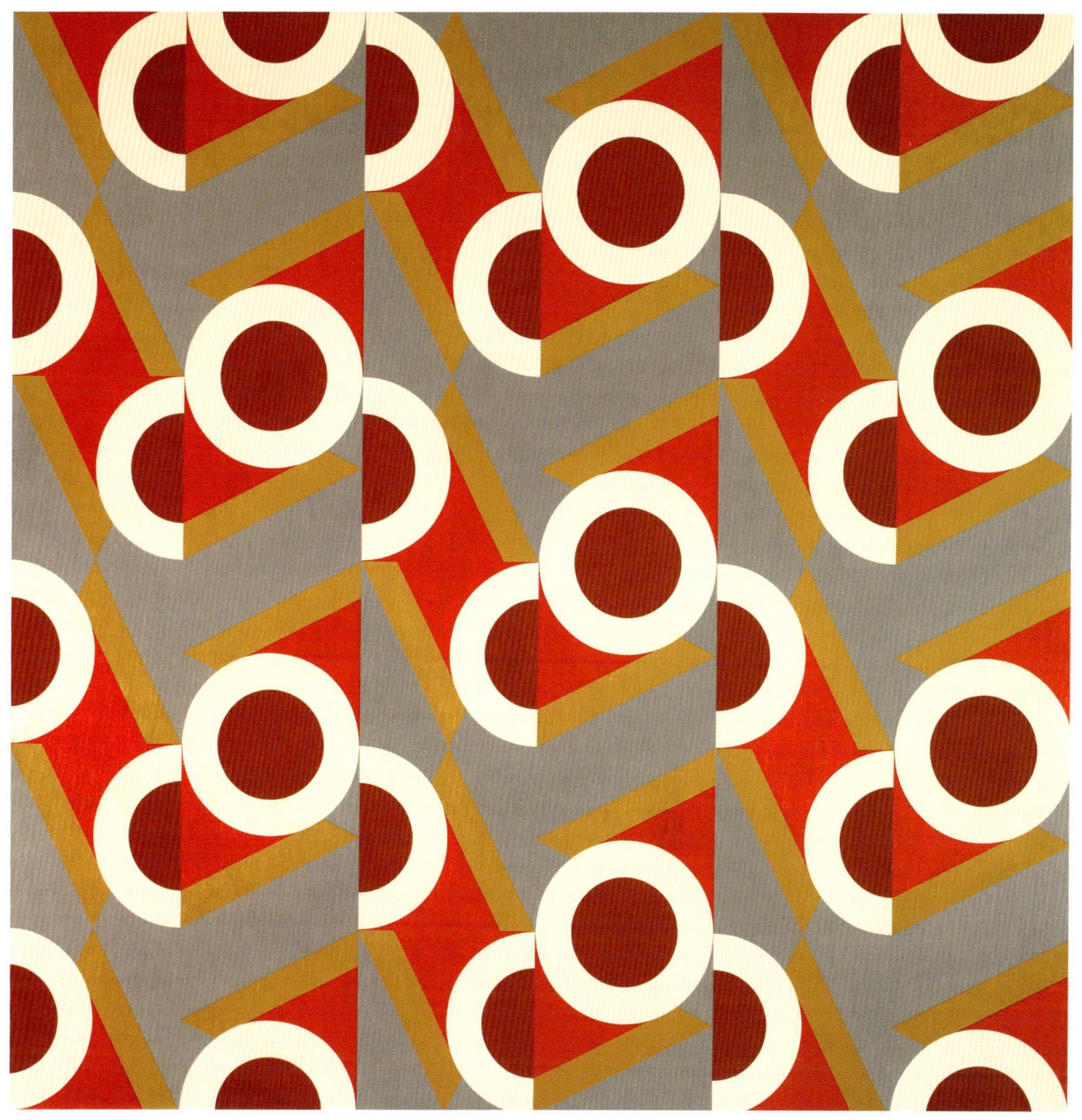

38 **#8**

1985
oil on canvas
60 x 60 inches
152.4 x 152.4 centimeters

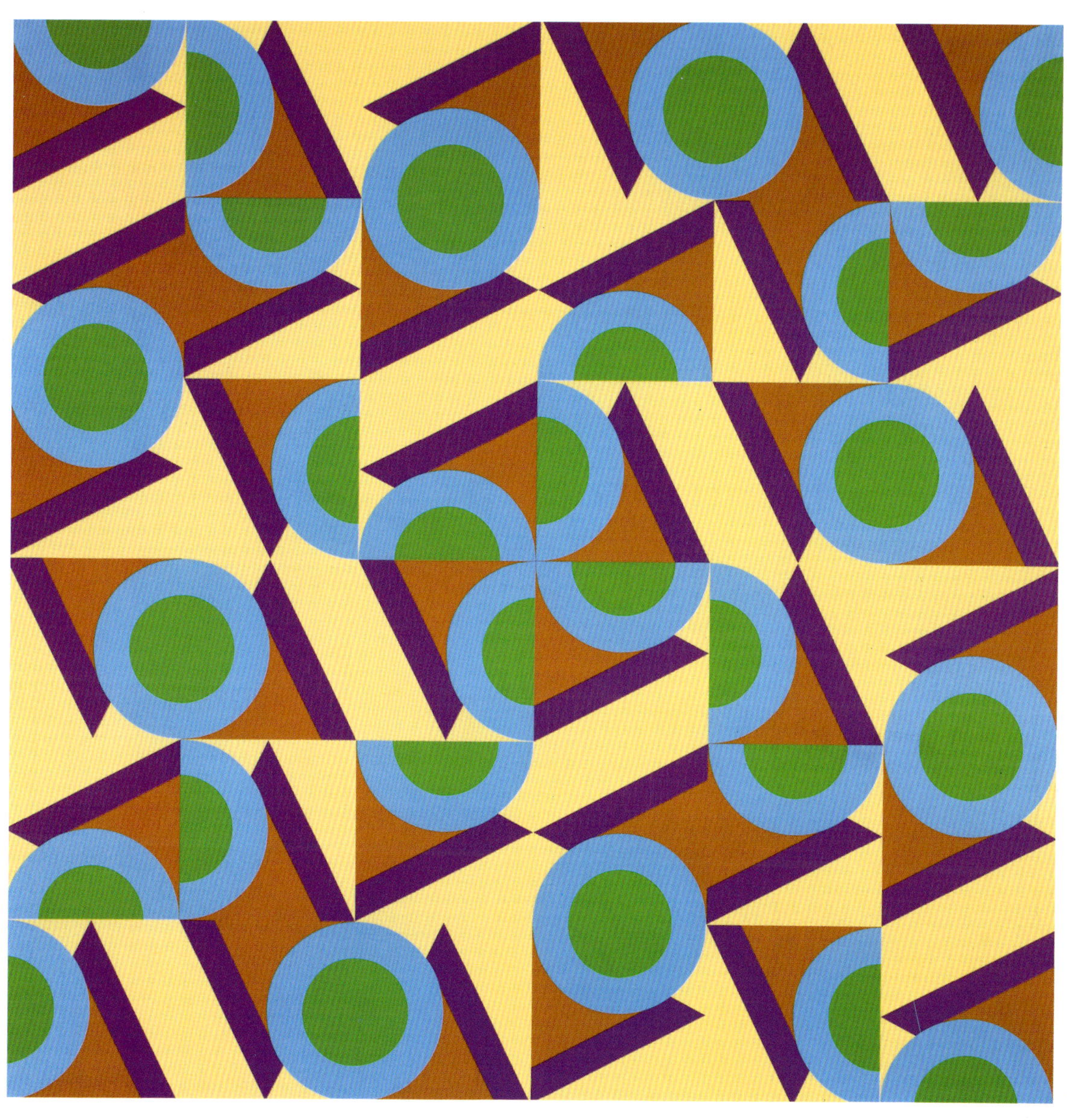

39 **#11**

1985
oil on canvas
60 x 60 inches
152.4 x 152.4 centimeters

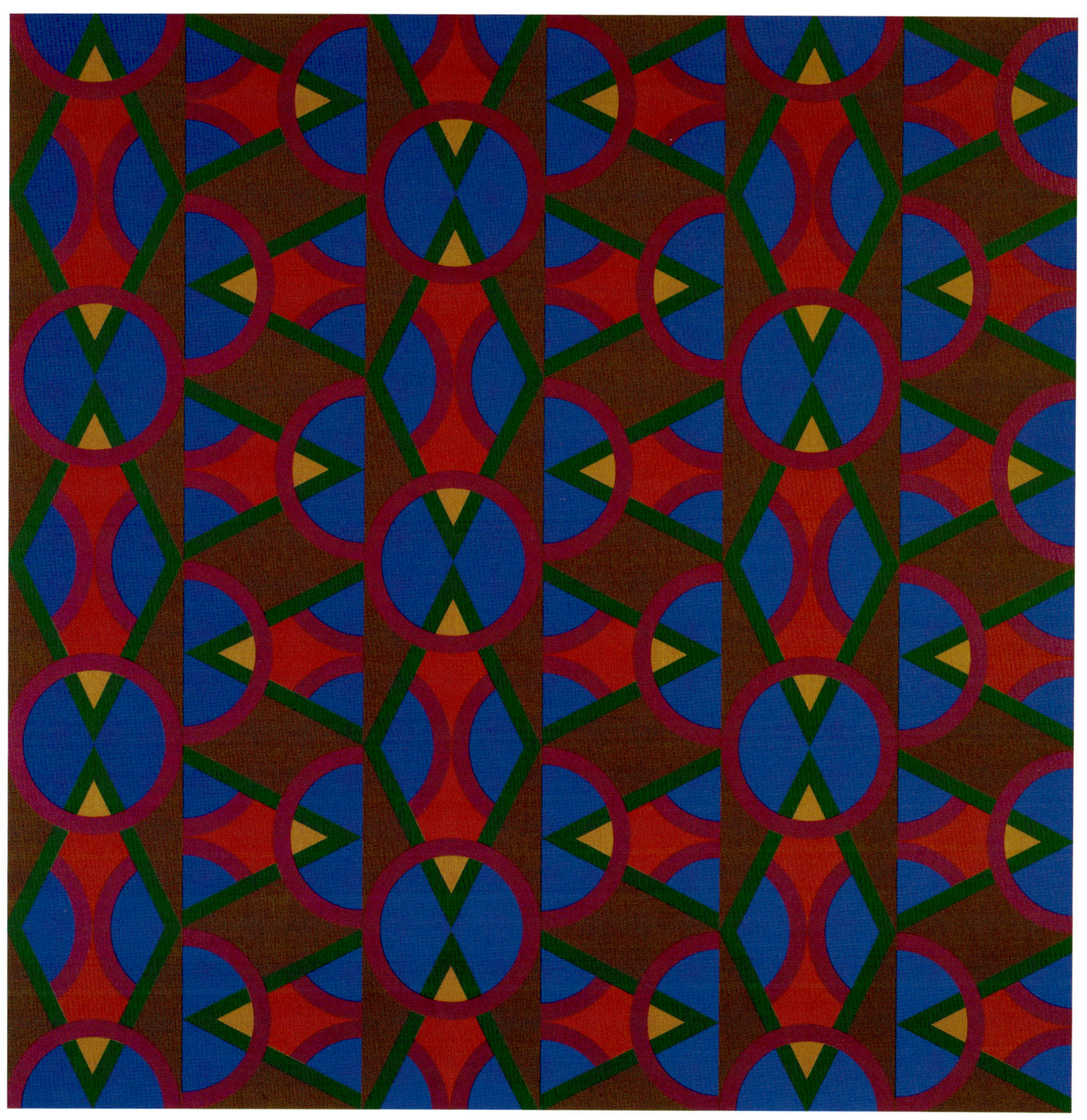

40 **#16**

1985
oil on canvas
60 x 60 inches
152.4 x 152.4 centimeters

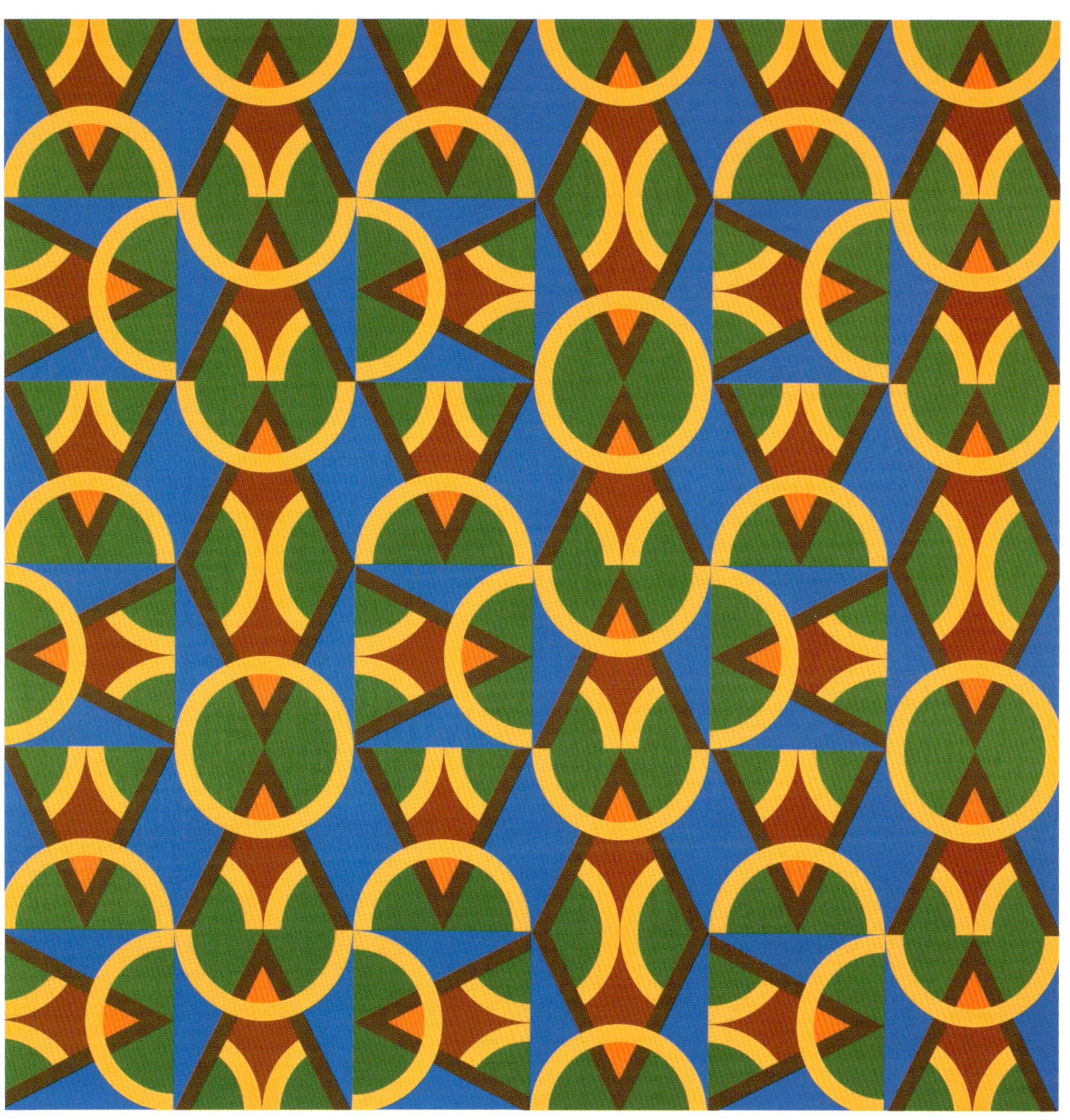

41 **#19**

1985
oil on canvas
60 x 60 inches
152.4 x 152.4 centimeters

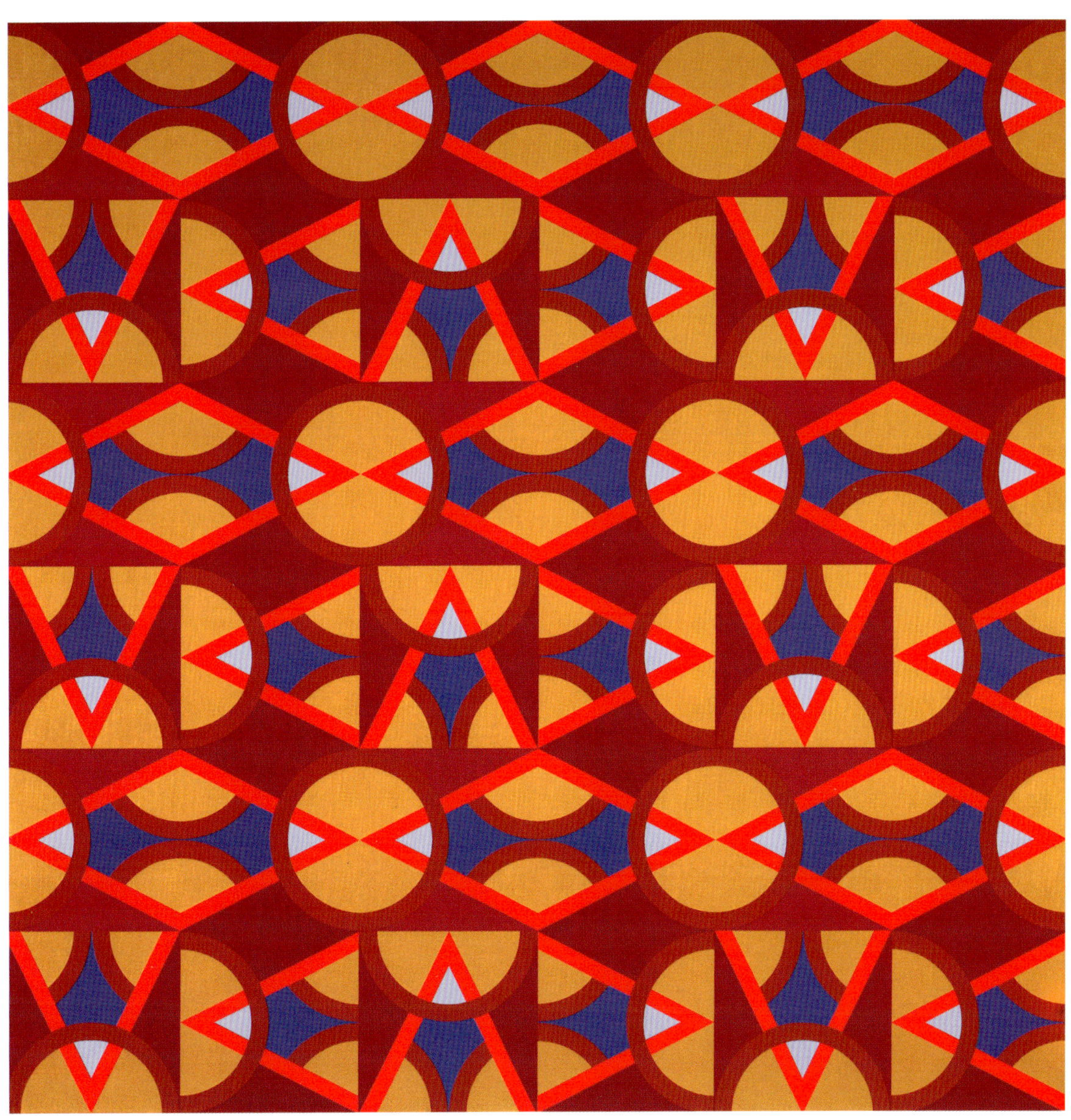

42 **#5**

1986
oil on canvas
60 x 60 inches
152.4 x 152.4 centimeters

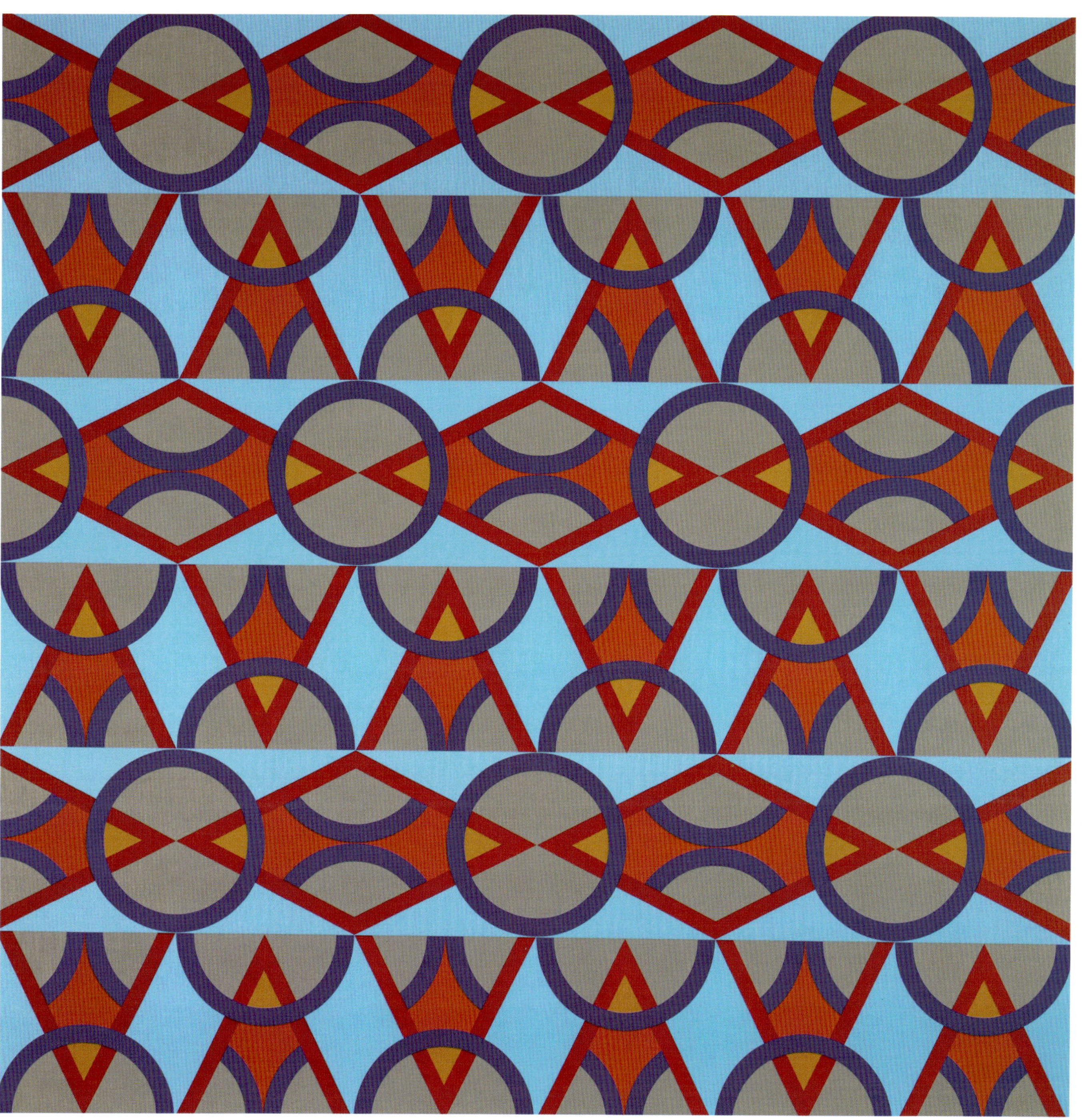

43 **#18**

1986
oil on canvas
63 x 45 inches
160 x 114.3 centimeters

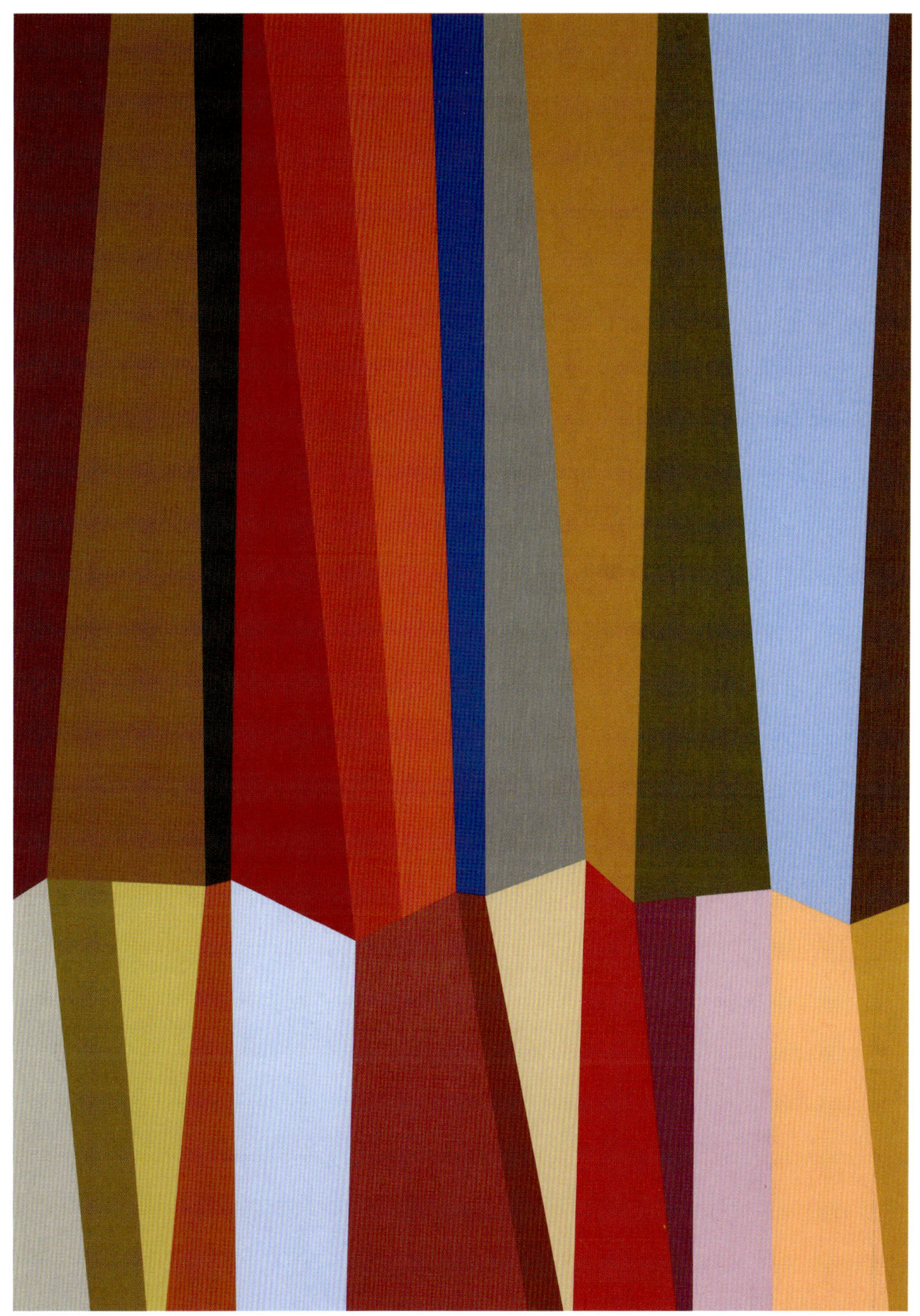

44 **#3**

1986
oil on canvas
63 x 45 inches
160 x 114.3 centimeters

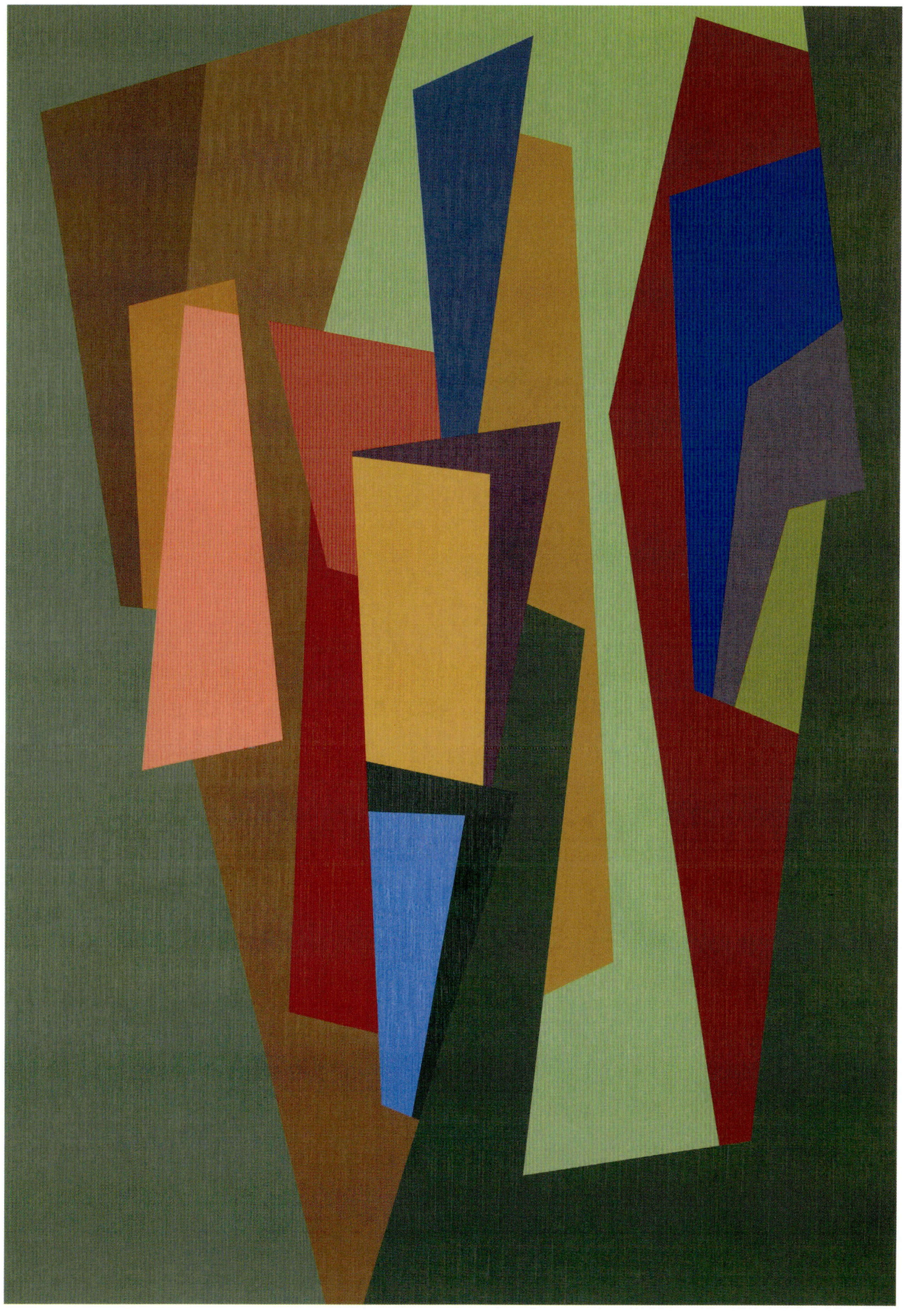

45 **#5**

1987
oil on canvas
40 x 40 inches
101.6 x 101.6 centimeters

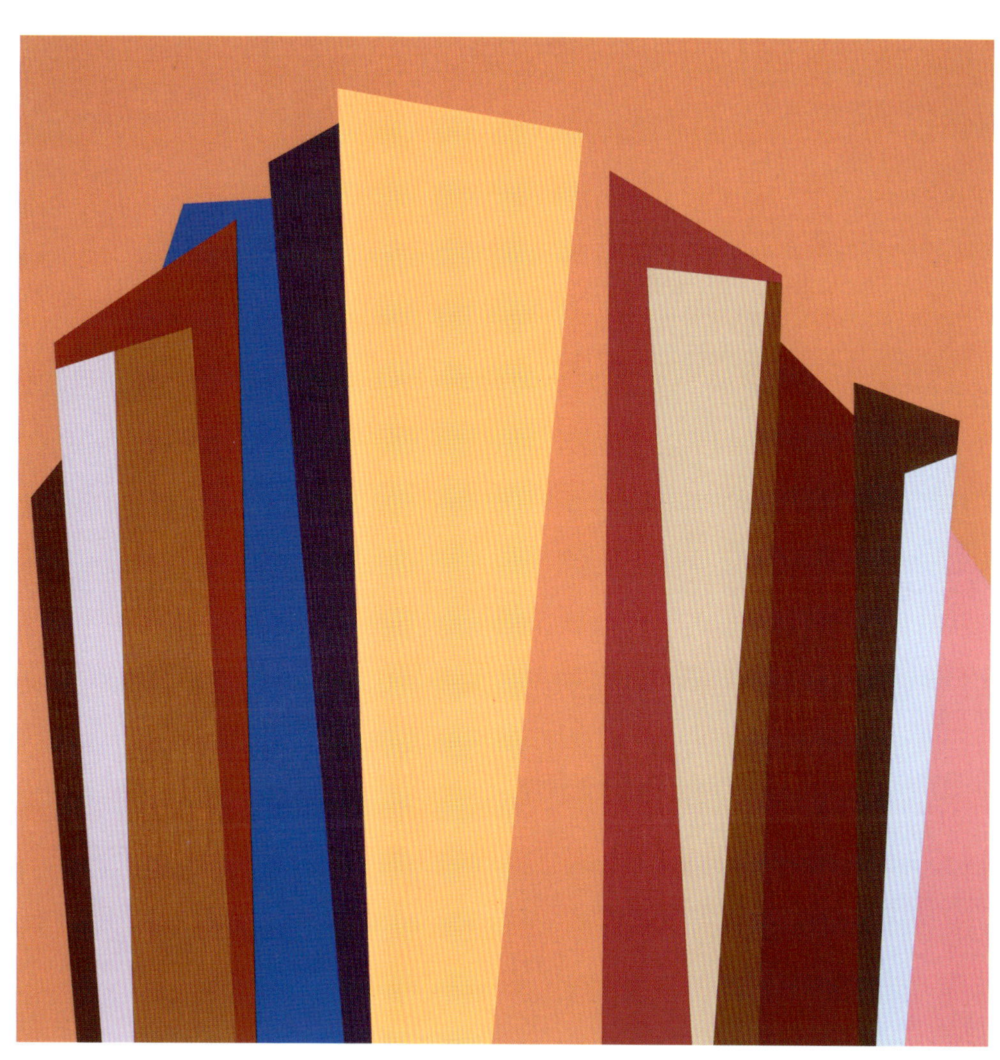

46 **#11**

1987
oil on canvas
63 x 45 inches
160 x 114.3 centimeters

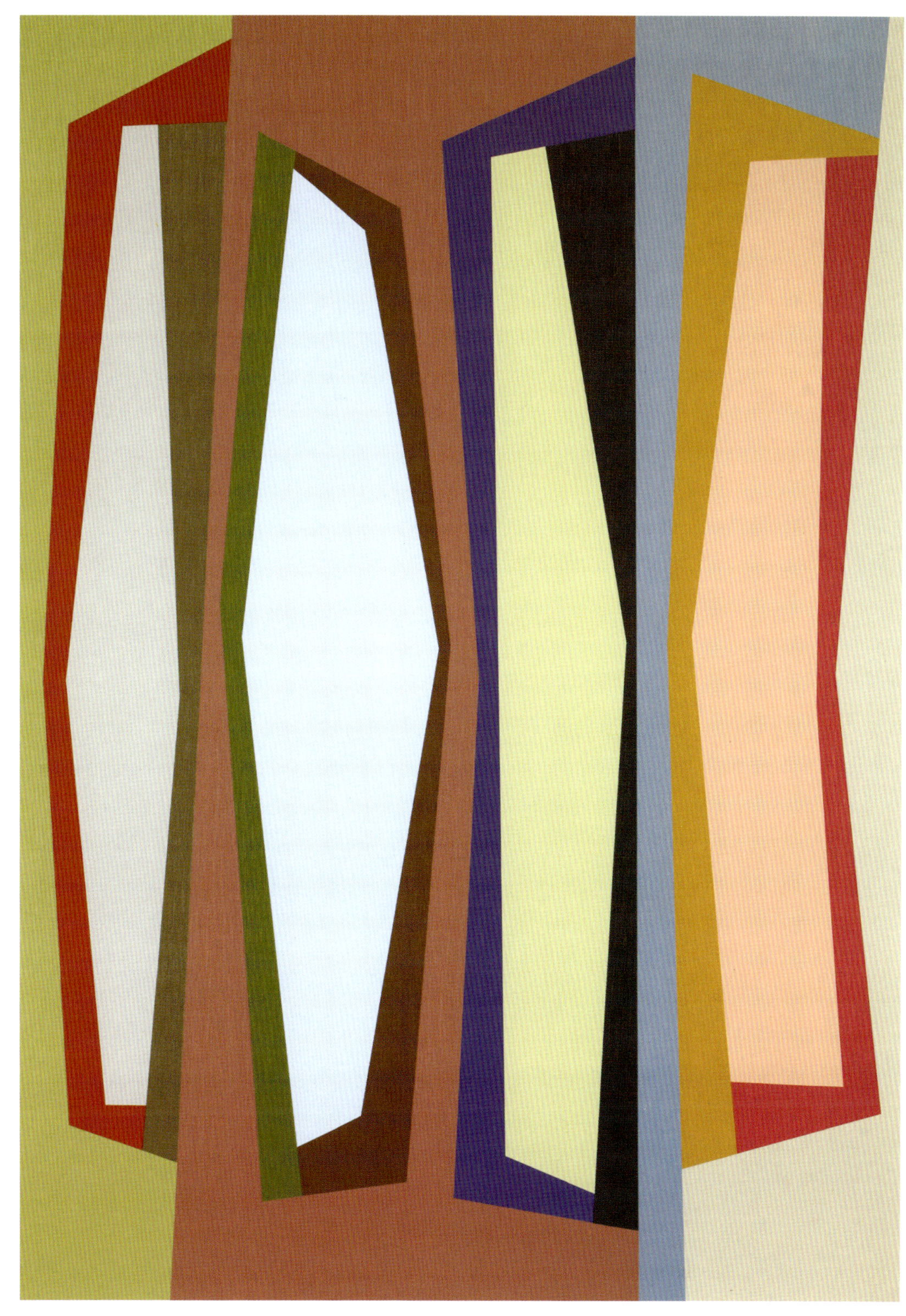

47 **#1**

1989
oil on canvas
60 x 60 inches
152.4 x 152.4 centimeters

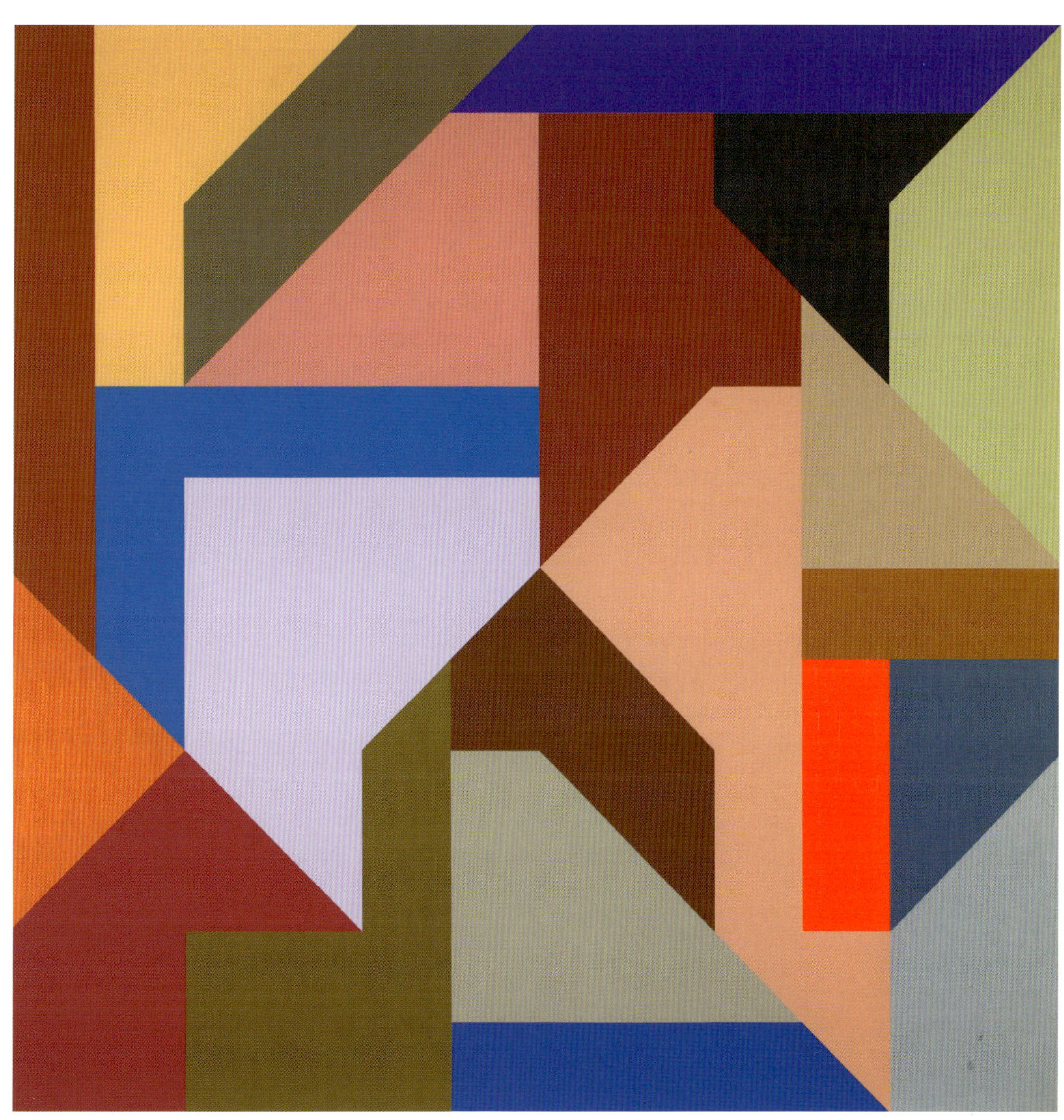

48 **#6**

1990
oil on canvas
48 x 60 inches
121.9 x 152.4 centimeters

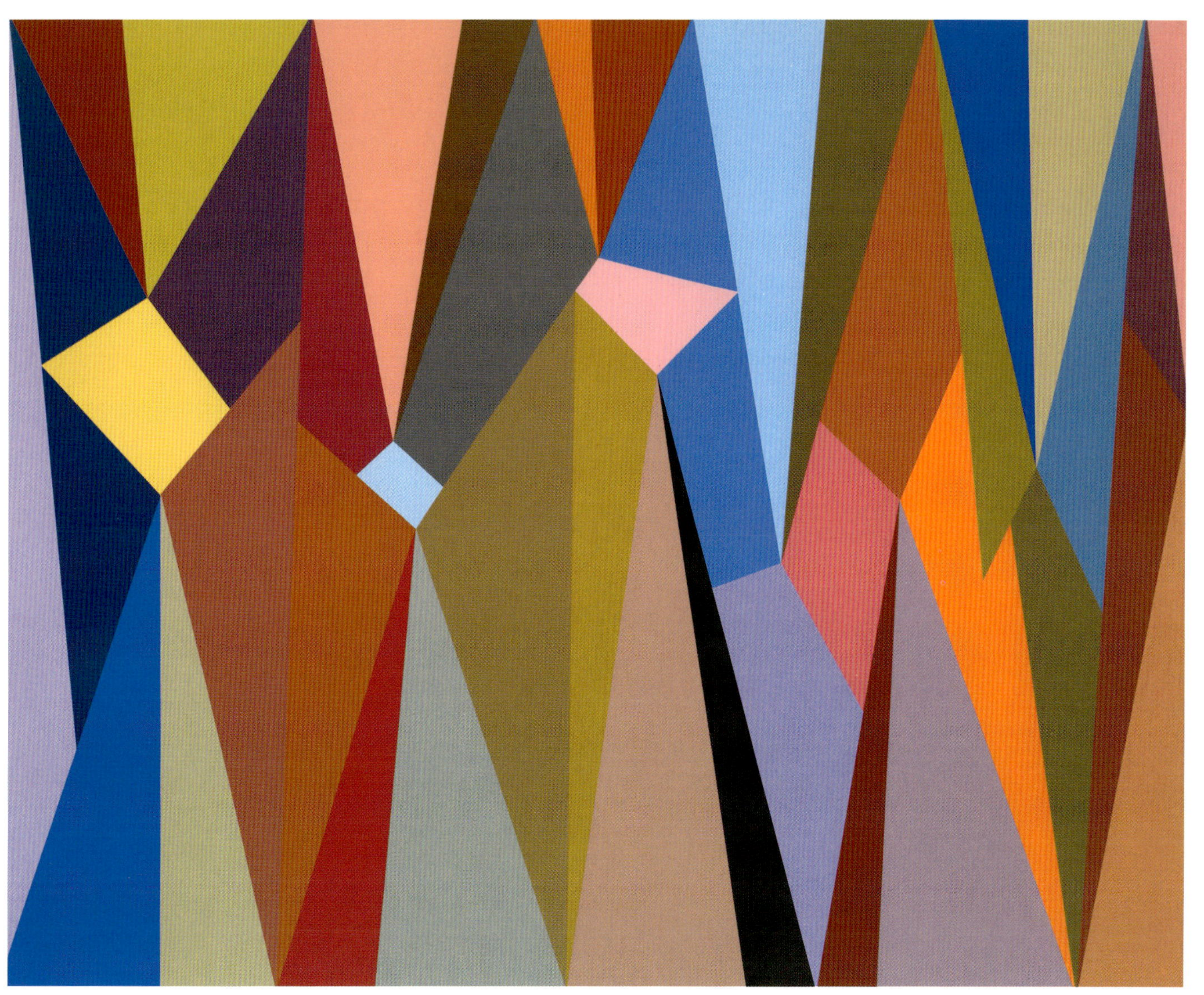

49 **#9**

1990
oil on canvas
60 x 60 inches
152.4 x 152.4 centimeters

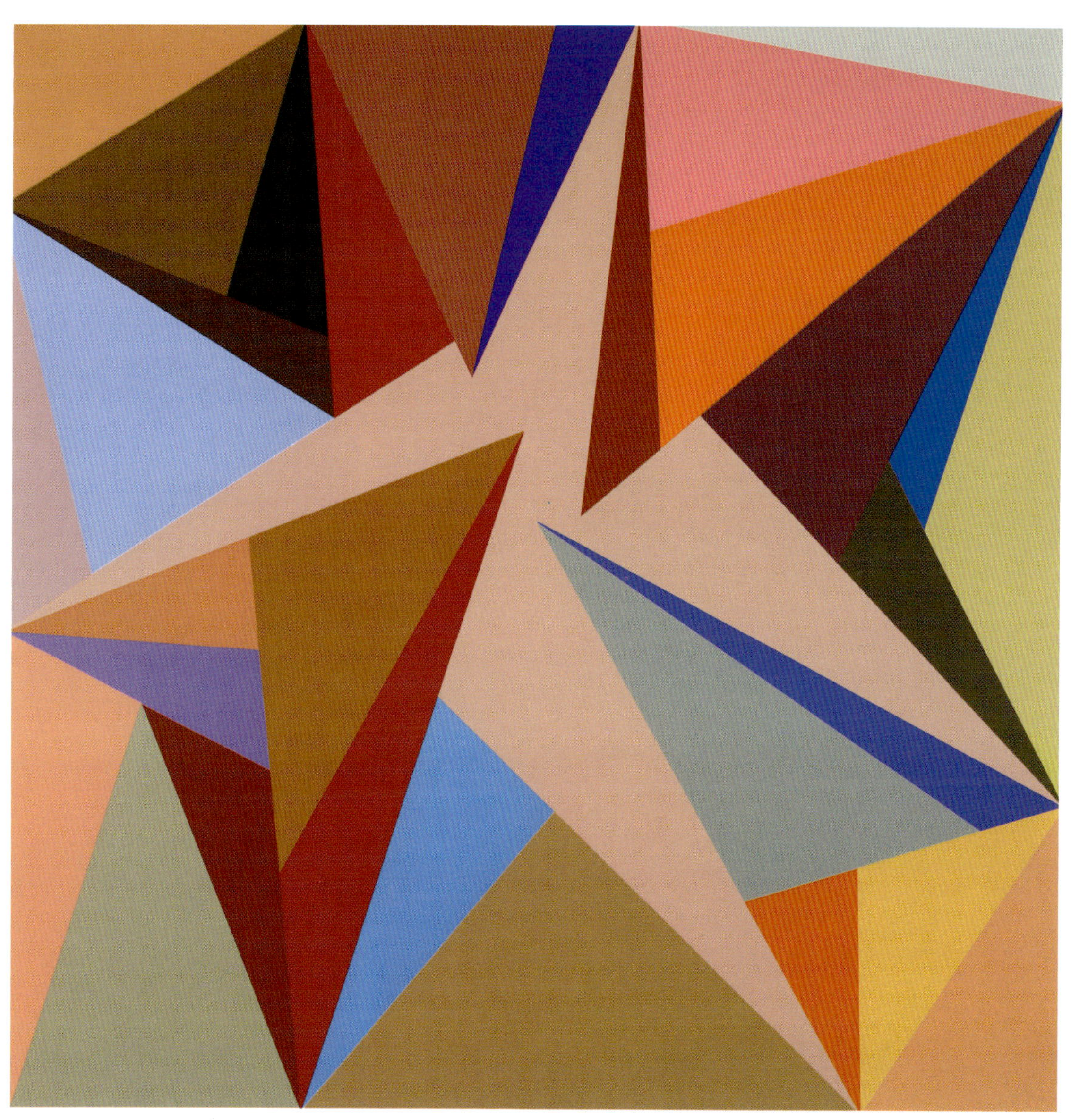

50 **#10**

1990
oil on canvas
50 1/2 x 30 1/2 inches
128.3 x 77.5 centimeters

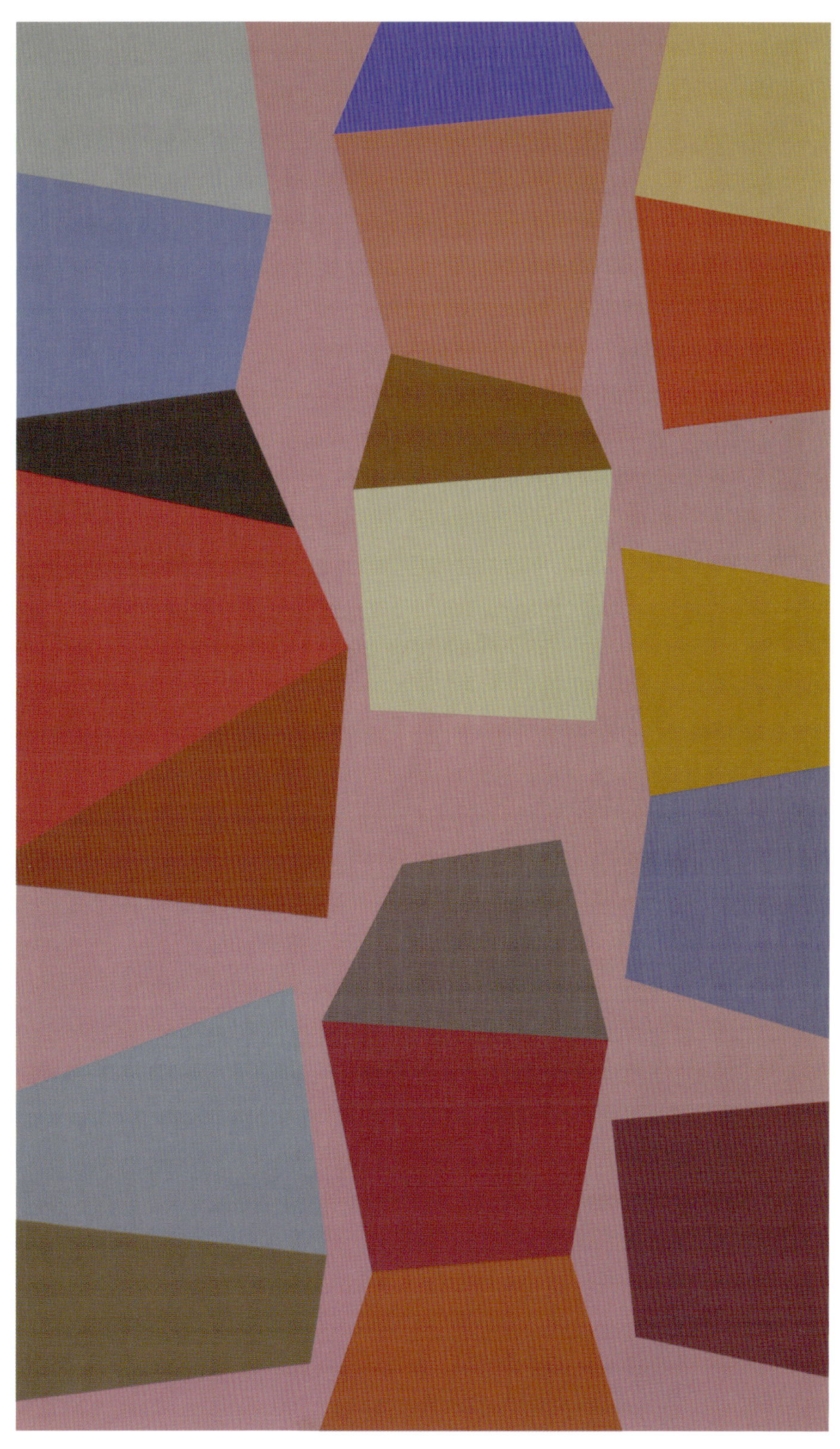

51 **#8**

1995
oil on canvas
44 x 56 inches
111.8 x 142.2 centimeters

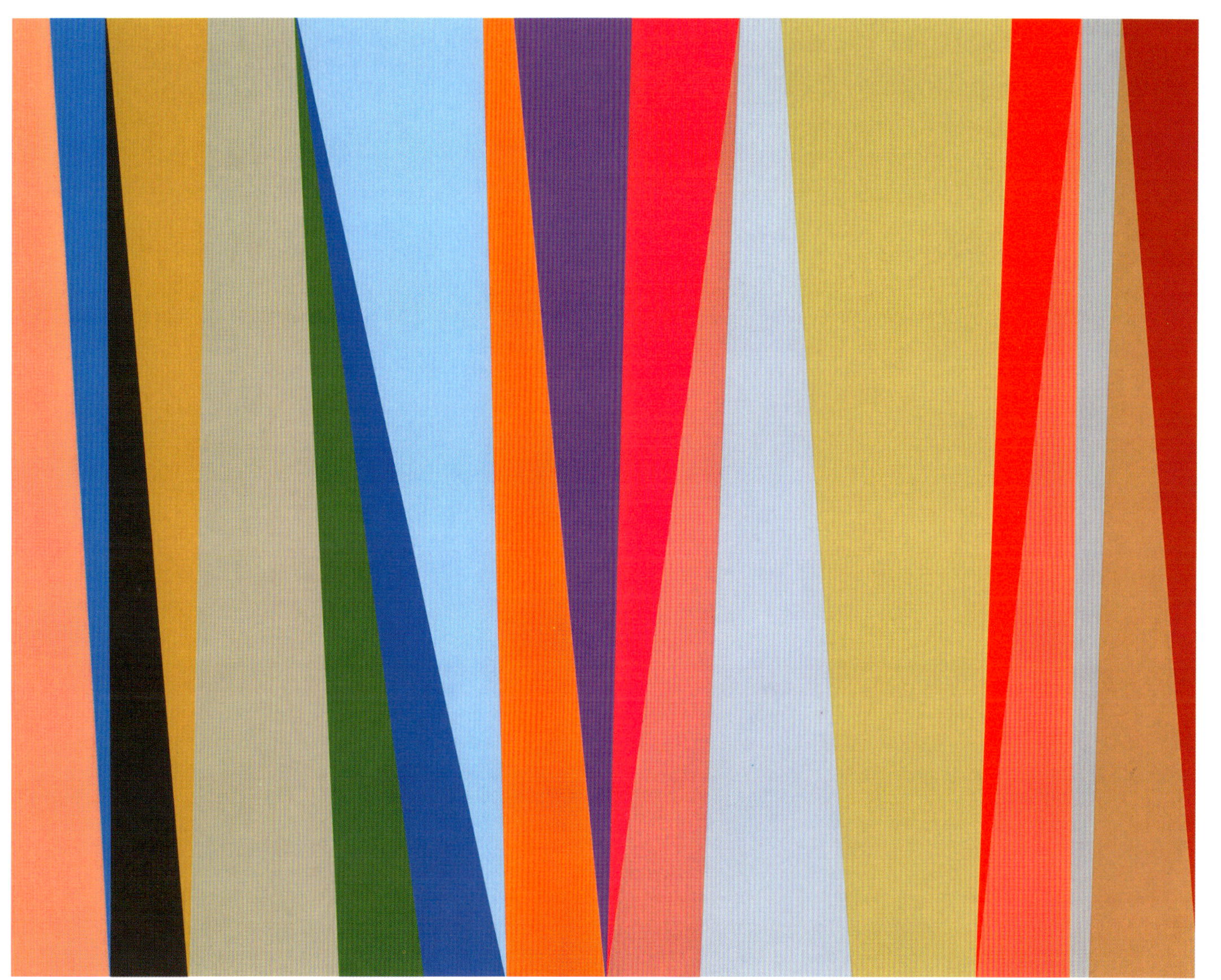

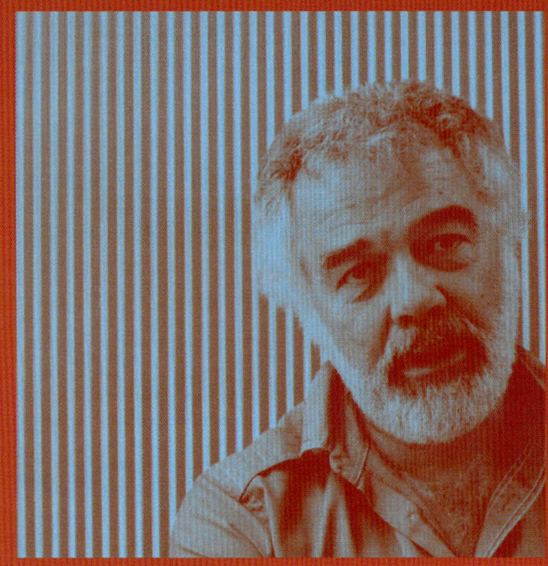

Karl Benjamin, circa 1970

solo exhibitions

2007   *Dance The Line – Paintings By Karl Benjamin*, Louis Stern Fine Arts, West
Hollywood, California.

Karl Benjamin: A Conversation With Color, Paintings From 1953 – 1995, Claremont
Museum of Art, Claremont, California.

2006   *Karl Benjamin: India Ink Drawings From The 1950's*, Lawrence Markey Gallery,
San Antonio, Texas.

2005   *Karl Benjamin: Drawings 1950-1965*, Louis Stern Fine Arts, West Hollywood, California.

2004   *Alphabet Series 1964-1965*, Brian Gross Fine Art, San Francisco, California.

Karl Benjamin: Paintings 1950-1965, Louis Stern Fine Arts, West Hollywood, California.

2003   *Stripe Paintings 1979-1981*, Brian Gross Fine Art, San Francisco, California.

2001   *(Mostly) Random Rectangles*, Brian Gross Fine Art, San Francisco, California.

Karl Benjamin: A Selective Retrospective, Cuttress Fine Art, Pomona California.

1998   *Paintings From The 50's and 90's*, Ruth Bachofner Gallery, Santa Monica, California.
In conjunction with UCLA at the Armand Hammer Museum *Sunshine & Noir*,
Los Angeles, California.

1995   *LA Artcore*, Los Angeles, California.

1994   *The Pomona Years: 1979-1994, A Retrospective*, Montgomery Gallery, Pomona College,
Pomona, California.

1992   *Karl Benjamin: Paintings 1955-1990*, Gary Snyder Fine Art, New York, New York.

1991   *Recent Paintings*, Fong-Spratt Galleries, San Jose, California.

Karl Benjamin: Paintings 1955-1990, Ruth Bachofner Gallery, Santa Monica, California.

1990   *A Ten Year Survey*, The Art Galleries of Claremont Graduate School, Claremont, California.
Ruth Bachofner Gallery, Santa Monica, California.

1989   *Karl Benjamin: A Retrospective 1955-1987*, Redding Museum and Art Center, Shasta
College Art Gallery, Redding, California. Also shown at the University of the
Pacific, Richard H. Reynolds Gallery, Stockton, California; California State University
Northridge, Art Galleries, Northridge, California.

1988   Ruth Bachofner Gallery, Santa Monica, California.

1986   *Recent Paintings*, Ruth Bachofner Gallery, Santa Monica, California.

Selected Works 1979-1986, Los Angeles Municipal Art Galleries, Barnsdall Park,
Los Angeles, California.

Hemmerdinger Gallery, Palm Springs, California.

Francine Seders Gallery, Seattle, Washington.

Chrysalis Gallery, Claremont, California.

1985   Chrysalis Gallery, Claremont, California.

1984   Hank Baum Gallery, San Francisco, California.

University of California, Santa Barbara, California.

1983   Chrysalis Gallery, Claremont, California.

Francine Seders Gallery, Seattle, Washington.

1982   Stella Polaris Gallery, Los Angeles, California.

California State University, Bakersfield, California.

Francine Seders Gallery, Seattle, Washington.

1981   Abraxas Gallery, Newport Beach, California.

Karl Benjamin: Paintings From The 50's, Pepperdine University, Malibu, California.

Shasta College Art Gallery, Redding, California.

Libra Gallery, Claremont Graduate School, Claremont, California.

Chaffey College, Alta Loma, California.

Francine Seders Gallery, Seattle, Washington.

1980   *Karl Benjamin 1970-1980*, University of Redlands, Redlands, California.

Cheney-Cowles Museum, Spokane, Washington.

Sheehan Gallery, Whitman College, Walla Walla, Washington.

Francine Seders Gallery, Seattle, Washington.

Tortue Gallery, Santa Monica, California.

1979   Francine Seders Gallery, Seattle, Washington.

1978   Francine Seders Gallery, Seattle, Washington.

Karl Benjamin: Recent Paintings, Tortue Gallery, Santa Monica, California.

1975   Chaffey College, Alta Loma, California.

Tortue Gallery, Santa Monica, California.

1972   University of Redlands, Redlands, California.

1971   William Sawyer Gallery, San Francisco, California.

Muckenthaler Cultural Center, Fullerton, California.

1970   Utah Museum of Fine Arts, Salt Lake City, Utah.

Jefferson Gallery, Los Angeles, California.

San Diego Museum of Contemporary Art, La Jolla, California.

1969   Mount San Antonio College, Walnut, California.

1968   Santa Barbara Museum of Art, Santa Barbara, California.

        Henri Gallery, Washington D.C., Maryland.

1966   Hollis Galleries, San Francisco, California.

1965   Esther-Robles Gallery, Los Angeles, California.

        Jefferson Gallery, La Jolla, California.

        Laguna Art Museum, Laguna Beach, California.

1964   Esther-Robles Gallery, Los Angeles, California.

        Hollis Galleries, San Francisco, California.

1963   Wooden Horse Gallery, Laguna Beach, California.

        Esther-Robles Gallery, Los Angeles, California.

1962   Santa Barbara Museum of Art, Santa Barbara, California.

        Esther-Robles Gallery, Los Angeles, California.

1961   San Diego Museum of Contemporary Art, La Jolla, California.

        Bolles Gallery, San Francisco, California.

1960   Esther-Robles Gallery, Los Angeles, California.

        Lang Gallery, Scripps College, Claremont, California.

1959   Esther-Robles Gallery, Los Angeles, California.

1958   Long Beach Museum of Art, Long Beach, California.

        Occidental College, Los Angeles, California.

1956   Jack Carr Gallery, Pasadena, California.

        University of Redlands, Redlands, California.

1955   Jack Carr Gallery, Pasadena, California.

1954   Pasadena Art Museum, Pasadena, California.

1953   Claremont Book and Art Gallery, Claremont, California.

        University of Redlands, Redlands, California.

group exhibitions

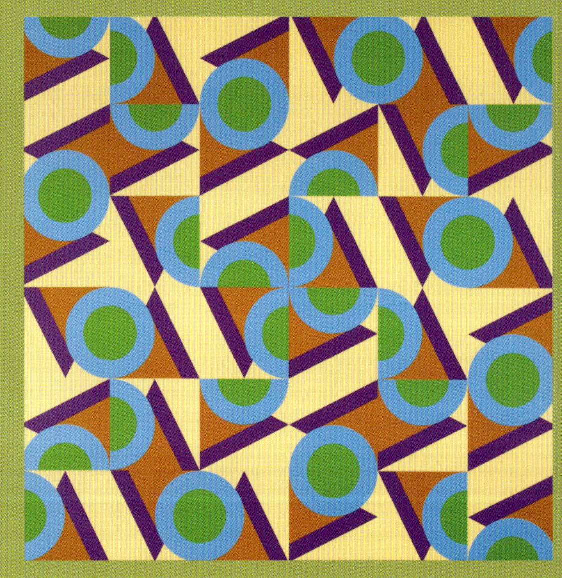

2007   *Birth of the Cool: California Art, Design and Culture at Midcentury*, Orange County
        Museum of Art, Newport Beach, California.

        After Image: Op Art of the 1960's, Jacobson Howard Gallery, New York, New York.

        Optic Nerve – Perceptual Art of the 1960's, Columbus Museum of Art, Columbus, Ohio.

        Painting < = > Design, Claremont Graduate University, Claremont, California.

2006   *A Little So Cal Abstraction*, Mandarin Gallery, Los Angeles, California.

        Driven to Abstraction: Southern California and the Non-Objective World, 1950-1980,
        (curated by Peter Frank), Riverside Art Museum, Riverside, California.

        Peace Tower (recreation of 1966 original) in conjunction with the Whitney Biennial:
        Day for Night, Whitney Museum of American Art, New York, New York.

2005   *Human Presence: Works from the Museum's Collection (The Geometry of Color/
        The Singular Body)*, San Diego Museum of Art, San Diego, California.

        The First 80 Years, Los Angeles Art Association, West Hollywood, California.

        Daimler Chrysler Collection: Minimalism and After III, Daimler Chrysler
        Contemporary, Potsdamer Platz, Berlin, Germany.

        Conversations with the Collection: A Selection from the Permanent Collection,
        Long Beach Museum of Art, Long Beach, California.

        The LA that Influenced My Eye, (curated by Barry Berkus), Sullivan Goss:
        An American Gallery, Santa Barbara, California.

        Beyond Geometry: Experiments in Form 1940's—1970's, Los Angeles County Museum
        of Art, Los Angeles, California.

        Twenty Years and Counting: An Exhibition Celebrating the dA Center for the Arts,
        dA Center for the Arts, Pomona, California.

        Collection Histories/Collective Memories: California Modern, Orange County
        Museum of Art, Newport Beach, California.

2004   *The Los Angeles School (curated by Dave Hickey),* Ben Maltz Gallery,
        Otis College of Art and Design, Los Angeles, California.

2003   *(Un)Taped: An Exhibition of Hard-Edge Paintings by Karl Benjamin and
        Mark L. Emerson,* Huntington Beach Art Center, Huntington Beach, California.

2002   *Ideal Abstraction 1955-1965, Karl Benjamin and Norman Bluhm,* Gary Snyder
        Fine Art, New York, New York.

2001   *Four Abstract Classicists: Karl Benjamin, Lorser Feitelson, Frederick
        Hammersley and John McLaughlin,* Gary Snyder Fine Art, New York, New York.

2000   *Vertical Chords,* Harris Gallery, Unversity of La Verne, La Verne, California.

1998   *Elusive Paradise: Los Angeles Art from the Permanent Collection,* Geffen
        Contemporary, Museum of Contemporary Art, Los Angeles, California.

        Convergences, The Art Galleries at Mt. San Antonio College, Walnut, California.

1997   *Eyedazzlers,* University Art Museum, University of New Mexico,
        Albuquerque, New Mexico.

        Generational Abstractions, Ruth Bachofner Gallery, Santa Monica, California.

        Geometric Abstraction 1937-1997, Gary Snyder Fine Art, New York, New York.

1996   *On The Edge of America: California Modernist Art*, Jack Rutberg Fine Arts,
        Los Angeles, California.

        California Focus, Long Beach Museum of Art, Long Beach, California.

        California Artists: Genres of The 20TH Century, Henley Gallery, Chapman University,
        Orange, California.

        Some Grids: The Theme of The Grid in 20TH Century Art, Los Angeles County
        Museum of Art, Los Angeles, California.

1993   *Four Abstract Classicist: West Coast Hard Edge*, Modernism Gallery,
        San Francisco, California.

        California: Art From The 1930's To The Present, San Francisco Museum of Modern Art,
        San Francisco, California.

        3 Artists: Common Origins, Different Paths, Carnegie Art Museum, Oxnard, California.
        Also shown at Kemper Gallery, Palm Springs Desert Museum, Palm Springs,
        California.

        Choice Encounters, Long Beach Museum of Art, Long Beach, California.

1992   Phinney Gallery, Palm Springs Desert Museum, Palm Springs, California.

        Selections From The Permanent Collection, Museum of Contemporary Art,
        Los Angeles, California.

        Turning the Tide: Early Los Angeles Modernists: 1920-1956, Laguna Art Museum,
        Laguna Beach, California. Also shown at Oakland Art Museum, Oakland, California; Marion
        Koogler McNay Art Institute, San Antonio, Texas; Nora Eccles Harrison Art Museum, Logan,
        Utah; Santa Barbara Museum of Art, Santa Barbara, California; Palm Springs Desert Museum,
        Palm Springs, California.

1991   *Post War Geometric Concepts*, Marilyn Pearl Gallery, New York, New York.

1990   *Geometric Abstraction*, Marc Richards Gallery, Santa Monica, California.

        Karl Benjamin, Steve Sschlichtenmyer, Art Gallery, The Claremont Graduate School,
        Claremont, California.

        Blueprints For Modern Living, Museum of Contemporary Art, Los Angeles, California.

1989   *Then and Now*, Ruth Bachofner Gallery, Santa Monica, California.

        A Decade of Abstraction, Seattle Center, Seattle, Washington.

1988   *The Linear Thread*, Irvine Fine Arts Center, Irvine, California.

1987   *California Paintings From The 60's*, University of New Mexico, Albuquerque, New Mexico.

        Desert Collections, Palm Springs Desert Museum, Palm Springs, California.

        Contemporary Prints By West Coast Artists, Francine Seders Gallery, Seattle, Washington.

        Pomona College Centennial Faculty Exhibition, Montgomery Gallery, Pomona College,
        Claremont, California.

        Insights, Laguna Art Museum, California and the initial installation in the Anderson
        Building, Los Angeles County Museum of Art, Los Angeles, California.

        International Contemporary Art Fair, Los Angeles Convention Center, Los Angeles,
        California.

        Four Abstract Classicists: A Look at 1950's California Hard Edge Painting,
        R.C. Erpf Gallery, New York, New York.

        Patterns—Culture and Perception, NBBJ Group, Seattle, Washington.

        Kisker Gallery, Scottsdale, Arizona.

        A California Collection, Cirrus Gallery, Los Angeles, California.

1986   *Ten California Colorists*, Shasta College Art Gallery, Redding Museum & Art Center, Redding, California. Also shown at San Jose Institute of Contemporary Art, San Jose, California; Palm Springs Desert Museum, Palm Springs, California; Montgomery Galleries, Pomona College, Claremont, California; University Art Museum, University of New Mexico, Albuquerque, New Mexico.

1985   *Color Forms*, Gallery at the Plaza, Security Pacific National Bank, Los Angeles, California.

        Drawings From The David Nellis Collection, California State University, Los Angeles, California.

1984   *Color, Color, Color*, Henry Gallery, University of Washington, Seattle, Washington. *A Focus on California: Selections From The Permanent Collection*, Los Angeles County Museum of Art, Los Angeles, California.

        The Twentieth Century, The SFMoMA Collection, San Francisco Museum of Modern Art, San Francisco, California.

1983   *Contemporary American Printing*, Shasta College Art Gallery, Redding, California.

1982   *Color In Contemporary Painting*, Henry Gallery, University of Washington, Seattle, Washington.

        Los Angeles Hard Edge, Tobey Moss Gallery, Los Angeles, California. Also shown at Fine Arts Gallery, Laguna Beach, California.

1981   *California Artists: 1940-1980*, Laguna Art Museum, Laguna Beach, California. Pacific Coast Museum Collections, National Museum of American Art, Washington, D.C.

1980   *West Coast: Art For The Vice President's House*, (paintings selected from West Coast Museum Collections), San Francisco Museum of Modern Art, California. Also shown at the Vice-President's House, Washington D.C.

1979   *Black And White Are Colors*, Montgomery & Lang Galleries, Pomona College and Scripps College, Claremont, California.

        Art Inc: American Paintings From Corporate Collections, Montgomery Museum of Fine Arts, Montgomery, Alabama. Also shown at the Corcoran Gallery of Art, Washington, D.C.; Indianapolis Museum of Art, Indianapolis, Indiana; San Diego Museum of Art, San Diego, California.

        Los Angeles Abstract Paintings, University Art Museum, University of New Mexico, Albuquerque. Also shown at University Art Gallery, University of California, Riverside, California.

1978   *A Painting Show*, Mt. San Antonio College, Walnut, California.

1977   *California: 5 Footnotes To Modern Art History*, Los Angeles County Museum of Art, Los Angeles, California.

        International Art Fair, Basel, Switzerland, and Cologne, West Germany.

        4 From California, Dorothy Rosenthal Gallery, Chicago, Illinois.

        Archives Of American Art: California Collecting, Oakland Art Museum, Oakland, California. Also shown at Santa Barbara Museum of Art, Santa Barbara, California.

        3 from California, Francine Selders Gallery, Seattle, Washington.

        Los Angeles Hard Edge: The Fifties and The Seventies, Los Angeles County Museum of Art, Los Angeles, California.

        35th Biennial Exhibition of American Painting, The Corcoran Gallery of Art, Washington, D.C.

1976   *Paintings and Sculpture in California: The Modern Era,* San Francisco Museum of Modern Art, San Francisco, California. Also shown at the National Collection of Fine Arts, Washington, D.C.

1971 *Pacific Cities Loan Exhibition*, Auckland City Art Gallery, Auckland, New Zealand.

1969 *Los Angeles Annual Art Exhibition*, Municipal Art Gallery, Barnsdall Park, Los Angeles, California.

1968 *Paintings From The 50's and 60's From The Collection of Gifford and Joann Philips*, University of California, Santa Barbara, Santa Barbara, California.

1967 *30th Biennial Exhibition of American Painting*, The Corcoran Gallery of Art, Washington, D.C.

Contemporary American Painting, The White House, Washington D.C.

California Art Festival, Lytton Center for the Visual Arts, Los Angeles, California.

1966 *85th Annual Exhibition of The San Francisco Art Institute*, San Francisco Museum of Modern Art, San Francisco, California.

American Painting, Virginia Museum of Fine Arts, Richmond, Virginia. *Contemporary California Art From The Lytton Collection*, Lytton Center for the Visual Arts, Los Angeles, California.

California Painters and Sculptures Invitional, Crocker Art Museum, Sacramento, California. Drawings, Gallery Dache, New York, New York.

Peace Tower, Los Angeles, California.

1965 *The Responsive Eye*, Museum of Modern Art, New York. Also shown at St. Louis Art Museum, St. Louis, Missouri; Seattle Art Museum, Seattle, Washington; Pasadena Art Museum, Pasadena, California; Baltimore Museum of Art, Baltimore, Maryland.

Art Across America, Mead Corporation, New York, New York. Also shown at M. Knoedler & Co., New York, New York; Toledo Museum of Art, Toledo, Ohio; Cleveland Institute of Art, Cleveland, Ohio; Wadsworth Atheneum, Hartford, Connecticut; Contemporary Arts Center, Cincinnati, Ohio; Isaac Delgado Museum, New Orleans, Louisiana; Commercial Museum, Philadelphia, Pennsylvania.

The Colorists: 1950-1965, San Francisco Museum of Modern Art, San Francisco, California.

California Artists, Witte Memorial Museum, San Antonio, Texas.

Survey of Contemporary Art, J.B. Speed Art Museum, Louisville, Kentucky.

Denver Museum Annual, Denver Art Museum, Denver, Colorado.

1964 *New Accessions, USA*, Colorado Springs Fine Arts Center, Colorado Springs, Colorado.

California Hard Edge Painting, Pavilion Gallery, Balboa, California.

Selections From The Asher Collection, University Art Museum, University of New Mexico, Albuquerque, New Mexico.

Painted Sculpture, Mount St. Mary's College, Los Angeles, California.

1963 *Liturgical Art*, Mount St. Mary's College, Los Angeles, California.

1962 *50 California Artists*, San Francisco Museum of Modern Art, San Francisco, California. Also shown at Whitney Museum of American Art, New York, New York; Walker Art Center, Minneapolis, Minnesota; Albright-Knox Art Gallery, Buffalo, New York; Des Moines Art Center, Des Moines, Iowa.

Geometric Abstraction in America, Whitney Museum of American Art, New York, New York. Also shown at Institute of Contemporary Art, Boston, Massachusetts.

The Artists Environment: West Coast, Amon Carter Museum of Western Art, Fort Worth, Texas. Also shown at Oakland Art Museum, Auckland, California; Wight Art Galleries, UCLA, Los Angeles, California.

1961 *Pacific Profile*, Pasadena Art Museum, Pasadena, California. Circulated in Western States by Western Association of Art Museums.

Paintings From The Pacific – United States, Japan, Australia, New Zealand, Auckland Art Gallery, Auckland, New Zealand.

California Artists, Carnegie Mellon Art Gallery, Carnegie Mellon University, Pittsburgh, Pennsylvania.

1960 *West Coast Hard Edge*, Institute of Contemporary Art, London, England. Also shown at Queen's College, Belfast, Ireland.

Purist Painting, American Federation of Arts, White Art Museum, Ithaca, New York. Also shown at Walker Art Center, Minneapolis, Minnesota; J.B. Speed Art Museum, Louisville, Kentucky; Everson Museum of Art, Syracuse, New York.

Museum of Art, Raleigh, North Carolina; Columbus Gallery of Fine Arts, Columbus, Ohio.

Annual Exhibition, Los Angeles County Museum of Art, Los Angeles, California.

1st Annual Painting and Sculpture Exhibition, La Jolla Art Museum, La Jolla, California.

1959 *Four Abstract Classists*, San Francisco Museum of Modern Art, San Francisco, California. Also Los Angeles County Museum of Art, Los Angeles, California.

New Talent, American Federation of Arts, Wichita Art Museum, Wichita, Kansas. Also shown at Time, Inc., New York, New York; Moody Gallery of Art, University of Alabama, Tuscaloosa, Alabama; Howard University, Washington D.C.

California Painters Under 35, Wight Art Galleries, UCLA, Los Angeles, California.

1949-1959: A Decade In The Contemporary Galleries, Pasadena Art Museum, Pasadena, California.

Kaleidoscope, Taos, New Mexico.

1958 *Arts Of Southern California Painting II*, Long Beach Museum of Art, Long Beach, California.

1957 *California Drawings*, originated and selected by Pomona College & U.C. Riverside Art Department and Hershel Chipp. Also shown at the Long Beach Museum of Art, Long Beach, California.

1956 *Art In Architecture*, Municipal Art Gallery, Barnsdall Park, Los Angeles, California.

1955 *Faculty Exhibition*, Pasadena School of Fine Arts, Pasadena, California.

10th Annual Newport Harbor Art Exhibit, Newport Beach, California.

1954 *14th Annual Invitational Art Exhibit*, Chaffey Art Association, Ontario, California.

Artists You Should Know, Los Angeles Art Association, Los Angeles, California.

39th Annual California Art Exhibit, San Bernardino, California.

1953 Falk-Raboff Gallery, Los Angeles, California.

5th Annual San Gabriel Valley Artists Exhibition, Pasadena Art Museum, Pasadena, California.

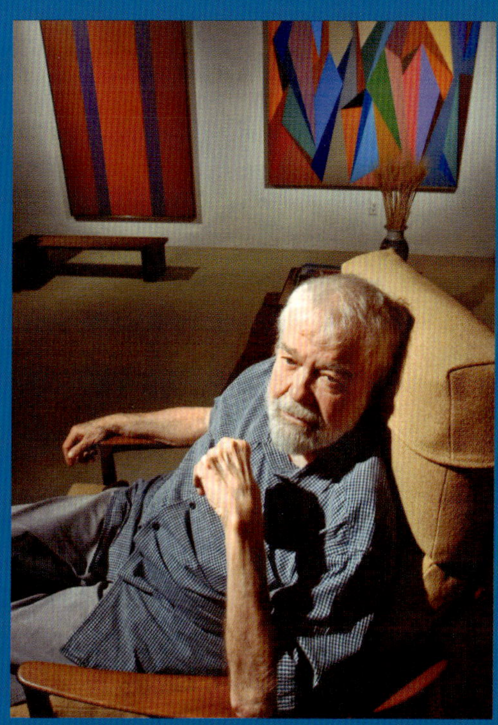

Karl Benjamin, 2007

public collections

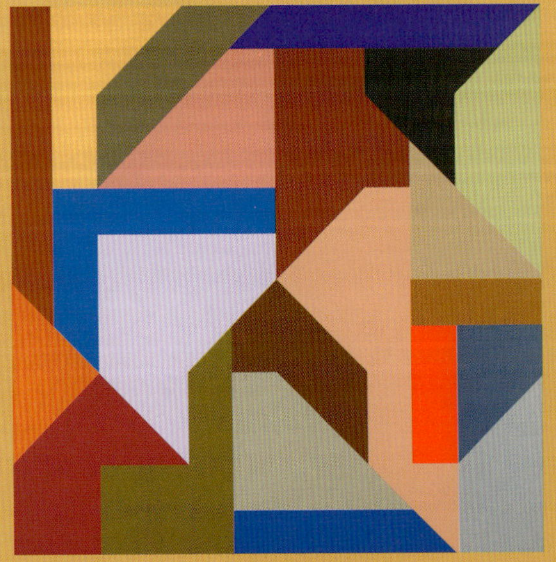

Art Institute of Chicago, Chicago, Illinois.
Baltimore Museum of Art, Baltimore, Maryland.
Cheney Cowles State Museum, Spokane, Washington.
Claremont Graduate School, Claremont, California.
Denver Art Museum, Denver, Colorado.
Fine Arts Gallery of San Diego, San Diego, California.
Harvey Mudd College, Claremont, California.
Henry Gallery, University of Washington, Seattle, Washington.
La Jolla Museum of Art, La Jolla, California.
Long Beach Museum of Art, Long Beach, California.
Los Angeles Institute of Contemporary Art, Los Angeles, California.
Los Angeles County Museum of Art, Los Angeles, California.
Mt. San Antonio College, Walnut Creek, California.
Museum of Contemporary Art, Los Angeles, California.
Museum of Contemporary Art San Diego, La Jolla, California.
Museum of Modern Art, Haifa, Israel.
Nevada Museum of Art, Reno, Nevada.
Newport Harbor Art Museum, Newport Beach, California.
Nora Eccles Harrison Museum of Art, Utah State University, Logan, Utah.
North Carolina Museum of Art, Raleigh, North Carolina.
Norton Simon Museum of Art, Pasadena, California.
Oakland Museum, Oakland, California.
Palm Springs Desert Museum, Palm Springs, California.
Pasadena Museum of California Art, Pasadena, California.
Pitzer College, Claremont, California.
Pomona College, Claremont, California.
San Diego Museum of Art, Balboa Park, California.
San Francisco Museum of Modern Art, San Francisco, California.
Santa Barbara Museum of Art, Santa Barbara, California.
Santa Cruz County Museum of Art, Santa Cruz, California.
Scripps College, Claremont, California.
Seattle Art Museum, Seattle, Washington.
Sheldon Memorial Gallery, University of Nebraska, Lincoln, Nebraska.
Tacoma Art Museum, Tacoma, Washington.
University of Iowa Museum of Art, Iowa City, Iowa.
University Art Museum, University of California, Berkeley, California.
University Art Museum, University of New Mexico, Albuquerque, New Mexico.
University of Redlands, Redlands, California.
Utah Museum of Fine Arts, University of Utah, Salt Lake City, Utah.
Wadsworth Atheneum, Hartford, Connecticut.
Washington State University, Pullman, Washington.
Whitney Museum of American Art, New York, New York.

cover: Karl Benjamin, #17, 1970, oil on canvas, 56 3/4 x 56 3/4 inches, 144.1 x 144.1 centimeters

Photography and digital imaging: Michael Faye

Design: Lilla Hangay, Santa Ana, California
Production: Cross Blue Overseas Printing, City of Industry, California
Typeface: Dax
Printed on spco matte book
Edition of 7000

©Essay by Dave Hickey

©2007 Louis Stern Fine Arts, 9002 Melrose Avenue, West Hollywood, California 90069

Published by Louis Stern Fine Arts

ISBN 0-9749421-7-0
Library of Congress Control Number: 2007931329

Printed in China